Unlocking the Heart

A Guide to Pastoral Care

Will Riddle

1st Edition

Printed in the United States of America

ISBN 1495904113

EAN 978-1495904110

Contents

Acknowledgements

I would like to thank everyone who has looked to me as a pastoral influence in their lives. Most of what is in this book I learned from our time together, which has been really precious to me.

I would also like to thank those who have made a pastoral investment in my life, including Gus Miragias, Wayne Mitchell, Brian Miller, and Don Westbrook.

Kingdom Change http://kingdomchange.org is a teaching ministry part of the The Go Network http://thegonetwork.net If you have questions about this material, I encourage you to contact me personally at will@kingdomchange.org. All personal correspondence will receive a reply.

NOTES

Please note, that the term "counseling" as it is referred to in this book does not refer to professional therapy. It refers to spiritual guidance.

Any names, and some details, used in this text have been changed to protect the anonymity of those involved.

Introduction

Several years ago, a revival broke out in Lakeland, Florida. It was instigated by a young revivalist named Todd Bentley, and for a brief time it captured the imagination of the world, especially within spirit-filled Christian circles. It made the news, was broadcast on Christian TV, and people were flying in from all around the world to be part of it. Many were healed, saved, and delivered. Sadly, the revival ended when Bentley, who was married, was discovered to be having inappropriate involvement with one of his interns. He eventually divorced his wife and mother of his children to marry this woman. The revival was over.

Fast forward a few more years and another Todd has captured the imagination of the spirit-filled world—Todd White. Like Bentley, Todd White came from a drug lifestyle, unchurched and far away from God. Like Bentley, White is unconventional and sees dramatic miracles in his ministry. Like Bentley, White travels the world and inspires the church. But unlike Bentley, however, White has had the benefit of a true pastor and father figure in his life. This man helped him deal with the deeper issues in his life before his gifts and ministry got too big to contain them. White continues his dramatic ministry around the world to this day.

That's the difference that pastoral care can make. Bentley had struggled before the revival broke with what he called a "dark night of the soul," and while there were certainly many celebrity pastors around him, the true life-changing input of a pastoral figure to walk him through it and keep him back from ministry was not. This is less an indictment of Bentley than of the church system we have created where this kind of care is so rare. Pentecostal/Charismatic history is full of stories of men who broke through with God only to have their own lives break down.

We want it to become normal to have the kind of care that leads to long term health and success, but there are many reasons why this kind of care is the exception rather than the rule. Instead of thinking of pastoral care as something that only married couples and addicts seek, we need to begin to think of it as coaching that will lay the foundation for reaching your full potential in God. Instead of thinking of it as something done by a nice guy at your church, we need to begin to think of it as a core part of the gospel. Jesus did after all say, "I am the good pastor." (John 10:11). Pastoring is the art of unlocking the heart, and unlocking the potential of every person.

PASTORS AND PROPHETS?

Todd Bentley did not lack mentors. He was trained and grew fast because of the input of some outstanding leaders around him. What he lacked was pastors. And He didn't lack these kinds of figures by accident. He lacked them because in the parts of the Charismatic movement where people are the most committed and serious about God, we don't really even believe in pastors. What we value and get excited about are prophets. What prophets do is exciting and flashy. What pastors do is rarely noticed until the fruit of their work manifests years later, if it is ever noticed at all.

In addition, we believe that everything is supposed to happen instantaneously. We are very uncomfortable with the idea that that things might take time, that there might be a process of growth, not just instantaneous miracles. This is in spite of the fact that Jesus compares the Kingdom of God to a seed which progressively grows and to leaven working its way progressively through a lump of dough, and the fact that Jesus Himself was described as having to "grow in wisdom and in stature" (Luke 2:52). If Jesus Himself, God on earth, had to grow, the question is why are we so uncomfortable with the idea that things will take time?

We think it is unspiritual and lacks faith, but Jesus says that chasing signs itself is a sign of being unspiritual (Matt 16:4). We become puffed up by the experiences we have seen or heard about and therefore blinded about our true spiritual state (Col 2:18). We think that anything which involves wisdom which must be gained from human experience is natural and unprofitable, and we think that being a pastor involves only the application of natural wisdom. The fact is that Christianity is the process of incarnation – bringing spiritual realities to bear in the natural. Prophecy itself is simply a translation of heavenly revelation into earthly language. If information is of no value, then why even tell the person at all? In fact, when we prophesy we expect that the other person will receive information and take appropriate action. In effect, we expect that they will apply wisdom to the words we receive. Being a pastor is partly about becoming expert in this kind of practical application. It would seem we should value that more.

In reality, pastoring and prophecy are not in opposition, nor are they completely separate functions. They are both manifestations of the identity of Christ within you. It is not that only some can prophesy or only some can heal the sick. All may prophesy (1 Cor 14:31) and all are commanded to heal the sick (Matt 10:8). Why wouldn't all also have the capacity to exercise pastoral care? Pastoring seems to be the last function of the church that Charismatics believe should only be done by someone in a 5-fold office. In fact, if you have ever given advice to a friend, you have exercised a dimension of pastoral care. Dismissing the impact of speaking into someone's life diminishes your own impact and ministry. The skills of pastoral care are simply one of the tools that every Christian should have in their toolbelt of growing the Kingdom of God.

Secondly, the work that a pastor does is not unspiritual or devoid of the Spirit of God. When I prophesy to someone, they are essentially asking me to look into an unlighted room and tell me what is in the room. I seek God for revelation, and if I am tuned in, I can tell them one or two pieces of furniture in the room. When someone invites me into their life to provide pastoral care, however, they turn the lights on in the room, and tell me what furniture is there. Then when I seek God for revelation, I don't need to find out what is there. I can ask instead the meaning of what is there and what to do about it. In both cases, I'm using the same gift. It is just that in the second case, I am able to access a much deeper level, because the key information has been given to me already. A true pastor must flow in the Spirit of God, otherwise why would He have to give it as a gift? (Eph 4:11)

Pastors are divine gardeners. They partner with you to cause the revelation which God is releasing into your life to be profitable, to bring new and deeper revelation about who you are and how to grow in God, and how to interpret the work that God is doing in your life. A pastor is a supernatural actor who helps release your potential in God, not just a nice guy who gives you some advice when you are in trouble

STATE OF PASTORAL TRAINING

Let's assume you believe that pastoring is something important that you want to learn how to do. The obvious question becomes: if you wanted to become a good pastor, what would you do? Where would you go? You might assume that you could go to seminary – pastor school -- to be trained as a pastor. In the mainstream evangelical movement, this is exactly what most people do.

Seminary is considered the appropriate way to learn how to be a pastor, and the degree you obtain is the Masters of Divinity or M.Div. This degree is one of the longest Master's degrees you can pursue. It takes three years of full time study, equivalent to a law degree. If you go to a good seminary, you are likely to learn a lot about the Bible, various kinds of theology, Greek, and Hebrew. Throw in some church history, and maybe a course or two on leadership or pastoral care, and you are all now "ready to pastor." Then you will go back to the field, armed with all of this information and ready to do the work of the ministry, right? Well, not exactly. It only takes a year or two on the field for most graduates to begin to wish they had learned a lot more about dealing with people and less about parsing Greek verbs.

By contrast, in the spirit-filled church, experience and the power of the Spirit are given primacy. Class-wise, you might receive some less formal training at an in-house Bible school. This training will be more practical than seminary, but it is still likely to focus largely on training you how to think like a Christian, and not how to relate to and deal with real people. In the spirit-filled church, the primary method of pastoral care that everyone understands is prayer plus deliverance-related seminars such as Cleansing Streams, Theophostics, or Freedom in Christ.

All of these have their merits, but my experience in life, as well as pastoring others over the long term, is that prayer and seminars can often bring a breakthrough, but true transformation is something that is walked out over a long period of time. It requires a strong devotional life, a good church community, and a pastoral figure who can help you avoid pitfalls, identify roots, and walk you through to freedom. The Holy Spirit can do some things at the altar, and a lot in your closet, but without the loving involvement of another person who has the wisdom or perspective you need in the area where you are struggling, everything moves a lot slower, and you might end up in a pit which could have been easily avoided.

This isn't to say there aren't good pastoral caregivers. There are many, but they become so almost by accident. Neither the systems in the evangelical church nor the spirit-filled church themselves develop the kind of pastoral skills needed to help people over the long run. If you have a natural gift, good mentors, and the right kind of experience, you can become an outstanding pastor. The problem is that few people are fortunate enough to have all of these.

This book is designed to help fill that gap. Obviously, a comprehensive book on pastoring could fill many volumes. And my intent here is only to deal with pastoral care, not the skills a Senior Pastor who runs a church would need– many of which are completely unrelated to pastoral care. This is a booklet about counseling people through the Holy Spirit. It is intended to give you a model to work with that will help you as you work with others.

The perspectives in this book come from experience and the Word of God. They are not academic theories, they are just practical. This is a how-to book. The models in this book should give you a strong foundation that you can use in any church context, or alongside any other model that is in place in your church. They are orienting principles for unlocking the heart of those wounded who come to you for care.

Part I – Foundations

The Pastor's Heart

What do you think of when you think of a "pastor"? The leader of a church? A preacher? Someone with a friendly personality? A pastor may be all of those things, but fundamentally, Biblically speaking, the essence of a pastor is something else: a shepherd. This shepherd keeps watch over a flock, and if you are part of that flock, the shepherd keeps watch over your soul.

Being a pastor, therefore, is not about the ability to teach or build big things, or draw a crowd, it's about the ability to care for God's people. The goal of the pastor is to protect and corral the sheep so that they can grow into everything God wants them to be. This book is about being a pastor in that sense of the word: a person who helps others grow in God.

When you start to look for it, you find that Jesus teaches very extensively on pastoring and being a shepherd. I want to explore some of this and make it practical. Jesus says in John 10:11, "I am the good pastor. The good pastor lays down his life for the sheep." Perhaps you've never heard it that way, but "pastor" and "shepherd" are the same word in the Greek, so this passage actually teaches us the first principles of being a pastor.

First, to be a pastor, you must be like Christ. In not just any way, but in the specific way Jesus explains in this passage: You need the dimension of love which would cause you to lay your life down for the sheep. This is what Jesus did. He possessed a love so deep and profound that he found it joyful to die on behalf of the sheep. In order to be a true pastor, a pastor of God's heart and sheepfold, you must have this same heart — the heart that would gladly die for the sheep.

When you really think about it, that's a profound dimension of love—that you would lay your life down for someone you are trying to help. I would lay my life down for my wife or my children…but for God's often wayward children? That's another level. That's the mark Jesus sets though: a love that is so profound, so intense, that you would go to the cross to save them. Paul even takes it to another level when he says, "For I could wish that I myself were cursed and cut off from Christ for the sake of my brothers." Paul is saying he loves those who hate him so much that he wishes he could go to hell on their behalf. I've honestly never met anyone with love that strong, but that's what it means to have a Christ-love. I would do anything to save you if I knew it would work… that's the pastor's heart.

On a practical level, this means you really care for your people, not just from a distance, but like a life exchange. You love them the way you love your son or daughter—wanting the very best for them all the time, understanding their decisions better than they do, and most importantly loving them more than are capable of loving themselves.

When I enter a pastoral relationship with someone, that's what I feel. I feel an intense desire to save them from themselves, to show God to them, to demonstrate God's love to them in the body. My life for yours. I want not just what is good for you, or just what is best for you, but I want the dreams of God for you that you can't even see. But even first and before all of that, I want to be with you in the midst of your life. I want you to no longer walk alone, but to know that someone in your life loves you so much that they would cross the ocean to save you.

This means that to be a pastor is to be a Christ-figure in someone's life. I don't mean to be "the savior," but to be a model of the Savior, to live out in the body the depth and dimension of the sacrificial love of God. That means, I don't have my own agenda, I can't have a way that I want to "use you" in my ministry. My only agenda has to be that I want to break every bondage off you that has held you back so that you can be who God the Father has always wanted you to be. That's a major part of what a real pastor does. They show you a love so real and tangible that you see God. You know He's real because you've been loved at a dimension that surpasses anything human. Someone has walked with you as Christ would.

The first and most essential dimension of being a pastor, then, is love. Not just a general care, but a "go out of my way, drop everything I have" kind of love. Of course this kind of love isn't natural. You can't just conjure it up. It has to come from the heart of God and become real in your heart, and then in your actions.

When you begin to pastor people you will find that their emergencies do not come at times that are convenient for you or your family. They interrupt. They do not come in small manageable doses either. They overwhelm. But that's who you are now. You are God's firefighter. You rush into the burning building of people's lives and you bring them out alive. And you don't wait for the call, all you need is to see smoke. When crisis comes, I will be there with you in it. Your life fell apart and there is no one to call? I'm on call. You're trapped in a situation you can't escape? I'm there to pry you out. You're running from God? I'm there to chase you down.

If you want to be a pastor, I mean a real "God pastor" you need that kind of sacrificial love. And you will know when you have it because it will compel you to do things you wouldn't do. You'll do them because someone else's life and walk with God depend on you. They are a sheep– they don't always know where they are going or where there is danger. You will do them because your life is no longer your own, but you have lain it down for the sheep.

Every Christian has the capability and calling to pastor others to some extent or another—the call to love people in that degree—but until you develop this kind of "out of the way" love, you will be very limited in how much you can help others. Some of us have had life experiences that keep us from wanting to or being able to connect well with others. You will need to be healed of these before you can do much in the realm of pastoral care. But the first step in that process is recognizing that you're supposed to develop healthy connections. Perhaps this book will help you by learning about what it looks like to care for others practically speaking.

Decide in your heart that others matter enough for you to get involved, even if it is inconvenient. Start looking outside of yourself and thinking about the needs and concerns of others. You might have to break some inner barriers which tell you that you "shouldn't get involved." In fact, what Jesus teaches us in the parable of the Good Samaritan is that it is religious people who do not like to get involved. The true heart of God jumps in just like the Good Samaritan did, and like Jesus did over and over in His ministry.

It's really that simple. We're going to look at a variety of techniques and principles in this book, but before any of that, beneath it all, you just need love, the Jesus kind of love.

1. In general, how emotionally connected do you feel to other people? When other people are struggling do you feel the urge to get involved and help them?

2. Can you think about a time in the last year when you went out of your way to help someone else?

3. How do you handle interruptions? Do relationships take priority or does what you are doing at the moment take priority? Look at your text message and phone call log. Do you tend to stop your life to respond, delay responding, or ignore messages?

4. Think about the people closest to you. When they are having difficulty, are you they one they call? If not, why do you think not?

5. Ask someone close to you for honest feedback about whether they would call you or not, and why.

When Not to Pastor

If you have a pastor's heart, one of the first pitfalls you will encounter are situations where you pour in endlessly but get nothing in return. And of course if you start to become good at pastoring, you will quickly have more people to help than you have time. Your friends will bring their friends, hoping you can help them too. So the question becomes, who do you help and when? The simple Biblical answer is that you help each according to his faith.

What does that mean? In the pastoral context, it means you help those who are hungry. You do not help those who will not help themselves. That may sound harsh, or counter to the pastor's heart we've so far explained, but helping such people is actually counter-productive.

To understand this better, imagine you have been in a very bad accident and need physical therapy to rebuild your muscles. Now when the therapist comes in, they will show you what to do and help you a bit, but having a therapist move your legs for you will not make them strong. In fact, if that is the only motion you do, it will make you weaker because you have to use your own muscles in order to grow. It is simply impossible for someone else to make you grow strength physically. And it is equally impossible for someone to grow strength for you spiritually. Now of course a good trainer or therapist can help you heal much faster and avoid pitfalls; they can show you the ropes. In essence, that's exactly what a real pastor does.

Therefore, one of the core realizations you need as a pastor is to understand that you by yourself cannot get anyone free. In fact, believe it or not, even God by Himself cannot get anyone free. It requires that person's hunger or faith to interact with the Spirit of God. Many people who are in a very bad situation want you to do things for them, but unless they are also willing to take a step, you must resist. The love of God in your heart cries out for them to be free, but you must not take action until you feel them pull as well.

This is a major pitfall for many pastors getting started. After awhile, every pastor learns this lesson from a few people who refuse to work and instead suck you dry. Maybe you yourself are breathing a sigh of relief right now. It's actually better for some of the people you are helping if you do nothing at all, and encourage others to do the same. Difficult people need to experience the consequences of their actions before they develop any true desire to work their way to freedom. So that's a rule I have in pastoring people. I don't do things for you, I do things *with* you. I am like a "matching grant." You are putting forward effort, and I will match your effort. I will not do more for you than you are willing to do for you, however. If you are in a place where you are obviously unable to swim, I will come to the rescue. But even then I'm looking for you to signal that you want it.

THREE TYPES OF PEOPLE

Some people are spiritually lazy. They are like the person who comes into your house and throws down their baggage and expects you to carry them up the stairs. They want you to do the work for them. If you do it, you will ruin your life and help them continue in bondage. What you are looking for is the kind of person who is ready to work hard to get free but need coaching. These are fewer and farther in between. Because both types of people "pull on you," you might not be able to tell the difference at first.

One way you can tell is to give them some kind of "assign-ment" when you first start working with them. I often give them my book to read, but it could be anything you think would help them—even something as simple as Bible reading. The point is, you want to see what they are going to do with your assignment. If they do nothing, then do not go back and do anything more. They do not have the sufficient desire to be free. Simply tell them, "Come back when you've done the homework." Some who seem spiritually lazy at first will surprise you and do it! But many will not return. These people are like the seed that falls on the path by the wayside. The seed never even makes it into their heart. The devil just eats it up. The good news is that some can be helped if you handle them correctly. They may return much later to seek help once their situation has gotten more desperate, and they see that neither you nor God are going to magically get them out. They will have to start to work and exercise faith. God will respond, and you will help them.

Another type of person is the person who is not teachable. A person who is not teachable always spins your words around into their own theory. They are always pumping someone else's teaching and their own method of getting free. They might even tell you how to pastor them! Jesus encountered lots of people that weren't teachable. He did not refuse to teach them outright. He simply spoke in riddles and reversed their questions on them. He did not invest a lot of time in them. His riddles and questions were designed to expose the condition of their heart — to get to the real root of the matter that they were not willing to listen or believe the things He said. So a person who is not teachable may have a lot of energy, but their energy is going to take them in circles because they are unable to hear what you are telling them. They think they "have it figured out" and want you to affirm them. They are running their own play instead of the ones you are coaching them to run. This is like the person with the rocky soil. You sow things in and it grows up quickly, but then just as quickly it's dead.

When you encounter the truly hungry person, however, you have found a gemstone. I will invest as much time in a hungry person as they can take. Move them into your house if you can. Take them on trips with you. Generally do whatever you can to feed this hungry sponge because they are going to take everything you say, and with their own effort and walk with God, bring forth fruit 30-60-100 fold. This person is the seed that falls on the good ground. What's funny about the hungry person is that they are often doing so much elsewhere that they demand less attention from you. You can easily overlook them and get dragged down by the lazy or unteachable person. Make sure you always return the hungry person's calls quickly and make yourself available because your efforts will be multiplied. Great will be your reward here in this life by seeing them grow, and in heaven through all the good they do.

In conclusion, pastoring is about having the correct heart towards everyone but knowing how to feed and invest only in the hungry. Pastoring the lazy person is the art of making sure they reap what they sow so that you and others do not do their work for them. The main thing you do is make sure they have things to do and that no one else is doing it for them. If you interrupt the process of reaping and sowing in someone's life it is counterproductive. They need those experiences in order to learn to not make the same choice again.

Your hope with the spritiually lazy person is that they learn the value of work and the pain of not working so they can become a true disciple. Pastoring the unteachable person is about giving them truth every time they come back with their schemes. You hope that they are able to hear something you say and start to learn to hear. If not, their plans will fail and that will bring them back to you for another chance to hear the truth. If they become humble through this process, they can be a good disciple because they have a lot of energy. It's just been wasted on the wrong things. For the truly hungry disciple, however, you simply pour in everything you know how. They will eat it up, come back for more, and move on with their own healthy lives when they've taken in enough.

Of course, some people are in between. If you are pastoring rightly, over time the lazy person will start to show some effort, and the unteachable person will start to ask real questions. You simply treat people like true disciples when they act like one, and when they don't you respond accordingly. It's proportional. Only once in a long while do you meet someone who is very teachable and very high energy. Most people are somewhere on the spectrum. Respond in proportion and according to each specific situation. Pray that they will move higher up on the spectrum to be a better investment. The good news is that some actually will. It might take several years, but the fact is that it is rare for someone to find a pastor who will get involved and really help them. That means that if they found you, they will likely come back to you. As long as you consistently reward positive, teachable behavior, and consistently "punish" negative behavior, over time, they can change.

Do not be discouraged about this process. Some people simply didn't get the right parenting growing up. Some refuse to be humble or work. Their failures are not your failures. You cannot make them work or listen. Just continue to love them with the heart of Christ and hope they will open up to truth.

Reflection Questions

1. Have you tried to make people get free before, who really didn't put in the work themselves? How did that work out? If you experienced burn out, why do you think that happened?

2. Do you have people who call you over and over, but despite your spending hours counseling them, stay basically in the same spot? What about people who really need help themselves but call you to teach you their pet theologies? What could you do to either provoke these people to action or stop calling?

3. Can you identify some cases where the person was really willing to do the work? How could you tell? How did that go differently from others who didn't?

4. After you got saved, did you have any particular bondages which led you in circles? What kind of counsel really got through to you? Did anyone "reward" your positive behavior or "punish" your unhelpful behavior?

The Root of All Problems

In the beginning, when God created the heavens and earth, he put Adam and Eve in the garden and gave them the tree of life and the tree of knowledge of good and evil. As we all know, instead of eating from the tree of life, which would have been eternal good to them, they ate from the tree of knowledge and brought upon themselves eternal death. This death came because of the separation it created from the only source of life: God. It created a veil upon their hearts which separated them from God, and separated them from others. This separation is root of every problem you will ever encounter in pastoral ministry.

Without a deep connection with God, every human being is running on empty. We either put other things in the tank in order to make it, or cope with the deep pain of having nothing inside the tank. This means that the goal of all of the ministry you do is twofold: first to restore the person's relationship with God, and secondly to restore their relationships with others. To the extent that you can lead the person in doing this, is the same extent to which they will be free. Jesus zeroes in on exactly this fact when he says:

> 'Love the Lord your God with all your heart and with all your soul and with all your mind.' This is the first and greatest commandment. And the second is like it: 'Love your neighbor as yourself.' All the Law and the Prophets hang on these two commandments.

Put what Jesus said in different terms: If you have a deep love relationship with me, and deep love relationships with others on this earth, you will fulfill everything that God has called you to do.

This kind of fulfilling relationship with God is possible because the veil which was put on our hearts through the sin of Adam is the veil which Jesus has torn. The torn veil is not simply a fact of redemptive history, it is an emotional reality. Because Jesus tore it, you are able to come into the fullness of God's presence.

Instead of being afraid of God and the punishment which your sin deserves, you can be open with God and receive cleansing for sin. The path to freedom could be thought of as a *progressive tearing of the veil* of sin to enter into relationship with God. Contemporary teaching neglects the progressive aspect of this reality. Growing in your relationship with God is being conformed to His image over time, removing sin over time, and developing a strong bond with Him over time.

This is the root of all freedom. It doesn't come from quoting scriptures, or having the right theology, or even being able to accurately diagnose your problems – it only comes from a living relationship with God where He is able to fill the empty tank. The depth of your relationship with God is exactly the same as the depth of your freedom. You simply cannot be a functional person without a living ongoing relationship with God. No amount of theology or human effort will fix that. Your work as pastor is to remove obstacles and show people how to develop a living relationship with God.

GOD AS FATHER

In order to have any kind of stable and successful walk in Christ, every person must first experience God's unconditional love. When Jesus tore the veil, that was exciting for God! We think it's about us having access to the Father, and it is, but even more than that, it's about the Father having access to us. He can come to your sinful self and not have to condemn you because of your sin. Instead He can come in His intense unconditional love.

Until someone is really receiving this love, they will always be up and down. Therefore your goal is to help the person discover and experience it. One of the most common blockages is some kind of religious attitude — what the New Testament would call being in "works." Any attitude which tries to get God's love by doing something, anything, is works. The number one first thing that every person needs is to receive the love of God deep in their heart.

I often explain God's love in terms of the prodigal son. He wandered way off into sin, far away from God, but God still loved him. We know this because the prodigal's father saw him while he was "still a long way off." In other words, the father must have been looking for him and with a heart of love. He did not wait until the son got home and apologized. He looked out over the horizon each day, hoping the son would come home. And then when the son gets closer, we see this kind of love demonstrated again because the father lavished love on him before he had any way of knowing if the son were repentant or not.

This is how God's love is. He loves you regardless of what you are, or are not doing. Until that's a deep and present reality, the person will be unstable because their relationship depends on them instead of on God. When they do well they will feel good, and when they do poorly they will feel bad. What is needed instead is to abide in the love of Christ continually.

Practically speaking this may mean you need to coach people to stop all of their religious duties such as Bible reading, fasting, witnessing, and formal prayer time. If the person is doing those things to get God's love instead of because they *feel* God's love, it's all dead works. Get them to reorient their prayer time around imagining God loving them, instead of asking Him for stuff.

Getting people to have this breakthrough is sometimes hard, and it may progress through stages. One major obstacle in people bonding to God is their believing God is permitting the problems and evil in their life. You will need to explain that God is not in complete control of everything. He does not will or even permit bad things to happen. He is not the source of problems; He is the answer to them. Sin is the reason that all bad things happen. Sin can be in the person themselves, in people around them, or just the general sin of the world, but the fact is that God is never the cause of evil. People usually are. What God permits is for evil people to be alive on the earth. He permits this because He wants them to come to repentance and not be in hell forever. And more fundamentally, if God were to remove all evil people, the fact is He would have to remove everyone.

It is very common in religious circles, however, to think that God caused or allowed something bad to happen, and as long as someone believes that, it can be extremely difficult to get them to trust God. Examples include things like:

- God did not kill your mother from cancer.
- God did not allow you to be abused as a child.

- It was not God's will that you lost your job or your family

For some people the truth of God's goodness comes easily, but others have chosen to believe lies about God because it takes responsibility off of them. If God is always good, then that means that the problem is with man. That can be uncomfortable for some people, especially if they have found comfort in blaming God. It is an art to bring them around the corner. Regardless, this is the first phase of all successful counseling, and so you should not move away from this issue until they are seeing things differently. In order to receive from God you must believe so strongly in His loving character that no human event can shake that belief.

I usually begin ministry in this area by doing an exercise designed to help people experience God's love. First I pray with them as the Spirit leads, with the goal of creating an atmosphere where God can touch them. Sometimes they may simply feel God's loving presence as I pray for them. Next I put on some worship music and ask them to imagine that God loved them perfectly, and that nothing at all could possibly stand in the way. I ask them to write down any obstacles or reasons why God can't love them, if they come up, and continue as an exercise in imagination to believe that God loved them. For most people this leads to a powerful encounter. For some people, you will need to work on the reasons they put down on paper before they will feel or experience anything.

You can build on this by asking them to revisit a time when God loved them. Have them imagine and revisit that time or place where they felt God's love toward them. Use a time of worship as a way of re-experiencing that closeness again. Encourage them to spend time there so that God's love can become real to them. Be responsive to the Spirit. Getting someone the breakthrough is an art. Nothing else really matters until you crack this false belief at the deepest level.

I find that one of the hardest groups to minister to in this way are people who have been abandoned or rejected by their parents. These people have a hard time understanding what love could possibly look like, and have projected onto God those deeply wounded feelings. Dad rejecting you looks so much like God rejecting you that it's hard to tell the difference. In addition, they may be asking in their heart, "Where were you, God?" A closer look at their lives, however, usually reveals that in spite of extreme darkness around them, God has still managed to reach through and do various things which show His mercy and care. The sinful people in their life may have made it difficult for God to reach through, but He still does.

Someone like this may need extended work in this area. I like to help the person reinterpret their life events in light of God's love. A person like this will often interpret every negative event as God not loving them, and ignore every positive event where He does show them love. I want them to actually see how His love is active and always has been in their lives. A good example of this is someone I met recently whose mother was violently raped, and he was the result. Because of this rape, his mother did not want him, and of course his father was completely out of the picture. This led to him feeling very bitter about his childhood. When we started to ask God how He had been present in this man's life, a different picture emerged:

- His grandmother had prevented his mother from getting an abortion, or killing him before he was born.

- God had protected him several times growing up when he could or should have been killed.

- God sent a prophet to him while he was in prison to speak a new future over him.

A better way to describe this man's life was that God saved him, kept him from harm's way, and reached out to him in the darkest of situations. Those around him who didn't know God or love him made his life much harder, but it didn't stop God from using every possible means to reach out.

MEETING GOD AT THE CROSS

Although God's love is unconditional, having a relationship with Him involves dealing with sin. This means that growing in relationship with God involves taking responsibility and exposing sin to God so that He can remove it. It is through the love relationship that He progressively exchanges beauty for ashes and changes your identity. As a pastor, this means coaching people to bring their stuff into the light and presence of God. Just as Adam and Eve had to get naked before God before they could be healed and transformed, each person needs to bring all of their pain, negative emotions, sin, confessions, etc, into the presence of God.

An illustration can make this more real. One way I have found that works is to lean back in my chair, close my eyes, look up, and demonstrate this so they can get a picture. As I lean back and imagine God's perfect love rains down on me, I feel free to be honest with Him about who I am, about my weaknesses and short-comings. He takes those away and gives me a greater dimension of his identity instead. His love will cleanse you as you bring these things continually into his presence. This is the cross, the place where sin meets God's love and forgiveness. Your goal is to bring every person to the cross. On the one side of the cross is sin, and on the other side is God's love. The cross is the place where this exchange happens.

Because of popular teachings, there are many people who talk a lot about God's grace or their identity in Christ, but actually are not changing. They have the one side of the cross — God's love, but not the other — sin. Because they do not really deal with sin, they are limited in how much they can grow. Thus the "in Christ" theology becomes a cover up instead of a foundation for a rela-tionship. Because this teaching is so popular, it is something I encounter frequently in counseling. The person confesses Scrip-tures, listens to mountains of teaching, and tells me how they know all the answers to personal growth, and yet their walk with God is clearly not working.

That's because the theology itself is a substitute for a relation-ship with God. Remember, your job as pastor is to help the per-son build a relationship with God. Through this relationship, His love and grace will flow and empower them to live a fulfilling and impactful life. I have a degree in theology and can talk the in's and out's as well as anybody, but over the years, what I have learned is that theology is often a substitute for relationship. Theology is necessary, because good theology gives you a basis for relationship, but it is no substitute for relationship.

Ironically, what is needed for the person obsessed with theol-ogy is better theology. Their doctrine is keeping them from getting honest with God and connecting with Him in a personal way. That connection happens at the cross, where real human frailties and failings encounter the unfathomable grace and power of God. If your theology has no cross, it has no relationship.

One type of person with this problem is the one who is always justifying their sin because "God loves me." In this case talking about God's love has no effect on them, it's just a cover. What they need is responsibility. This person is like a child who has never been disciplined. They do not respect or fear God in their hearts and are looking for a cover. Alternatively, they may be so afraid to "go there" with God because of all of the pain that they keep clinging to this false doctrine to keep them from needing to change. Until a person really surrenders and takes responsibility, the grace and love of God will have no effect. It is just an empty doctrine.

The sign of a person like this is that they have a very messed up life and keep talking all the time about God's grace, or their identity in Christ, etc. They do not show signs that they are surrendered to God's will for their lives, convicted of sin, etc. For this person, the first goal of your counseling is to cause them to see their sin. Only when a person sees their sin will the love of God actually mean anything. Jesus says that "He who is forgiven much, loves much," but if you don't really think you need to be forgiven of anything, then you aren't going to love much either.

These are the fundamental dynamics which underlie every pastoral relationship. You are helping the person to see their sin, to receive God's love, and to bring their sin out into the open where God's unconditional love can cleans them from it and lead them into deeper relationship. For some people a lot of heavy lifting will need to be done to really get them to surrender to God and get open about their sin. For others, the focus is really on getting them to have the "love breakthrough" so that they can be freed for the horrible burden of guilt they are carrying.

RELATIONSHIPS

Your relationship with God is the first foundation of health, and the second foundation is your relationship with others. The first and most significant relationship you have with other people is with your parents. This relationship is the one most responsible for forming your worldview of life. The way they treat you combined with the way that you process the way they treat you is what forms your "emotional operating system" through which you will process all other human interactions.

Sin prevents us from experiencing God face to face in this life. The closest thing most people have to experiencing God is when they encounter other people, since other people are made in the image of God. But an image is only a copy or representation, it is not the real thing. A human relationship can be very satisfying, but without God, it can only go so far. In fact, in romantic relationships it is common for us to try to make the other person into a kind of god that meets all of our needs. But of course this fails and leaves us broken. It is the same way in parenting. Your parents represent God, but they are only human, not God Himself. Furthermore, you were also born with sin, and therefore no one grows up perfectly. It is only when you are born again and fathered by God Himself that you can experience true wholeness.

Dealing with human relationships is therefore fundamental to the pastoring process in two ways. The first part is historical: you must deal with the relationships and experiences which led the person to interpret the world the way they do. The second part is contemporary: you must deal with their existing relationships, which are often a significant source of difficulty. And the two are connected. Usually the historical relationships do a lot to shape the contemporary relationships. If a person was abused, they often grow up with an emotional worldview which leads them either to be abused more or to abuse others. The goal of the pastor is to bring God into the picture and help the person heal the past, reinterpret the world, and develop healthy relationships now

An ongoing relationship is like an emotional pipe directly into a person. If a relationship is healthy, that pipe continually feeds positive things into the person's life, but if the relationship is unhealthy it is like an oil spill, continually bringing pain into the person's life. That means that trying to heal someone who is still in the unhealthy system is like cleaning up an oil spill while the well is still gushing oil. One of your goals as a counselor, then, is to help the person identify these unhealthy relationships and redefine them. In some cases this can be done through setting a new tone in a relationship – such as with a supportive spouse – but in other cases the relationship needs to be broken at least for a time, while the person redefines themselves according to God's heart instead of their history.

We have found this to be true over and over again in our pastoral experiences. People almost always need to change friends, and often need to get away from their family as well, even if the family is not all that bad. This is because the family is too powerful of a reinforcement to the old behaviors. It is much easier to help the person find a new role in a healthy system and bring that back to their family, than it is to try to change the family system while the person is trying to be healed. The same holds true for people with whom friends form their social reality. What is needed is a set of relationships where you can be seen differently and experience different emotional rewards.

I think of a friend of mine whose has trouble giving and receiving love. When he goes home to be with his family, the way they express love is to jokingly say things like "Look what the cat dragged in," or, "Oh man, look who's here now." These kind of statements are substitutes for truly vulnerable and direct communication. Even though everyone in the system understands that they are intended in a joking way, the words still have a way of erecting distance and leaving a bit of a scar – "Am I *really* something they cat dragged in?" It's important for my friend to hear directly that he is loved and valued, and to learn to say this back to others. As he practices this in a healthy relationship with me as pastor, and others in the church, he develops the skills and strengths to redefine the family system when he has to face it again.

Few people have the strength to completely redefine their relationship system on their own. Every time you begin to change, all of the other people in the system reinforce the role you used to play, trying to put you back into your place. And even when those around you are open to seeing you differently, it is very hard to believe they are seeing you differently. This makes changing inside of existing relationships three times as difficult. You have to change yourself, their perception of you, and then your beliefs about their perceptions of you.

The effect of relationships is also one of the reasons why group therapy can be so effective for people with addictions or other deep issues. Within a group of people who have similar struggles, you are all in the same situation. You are all trying to redefine yourselves. You may feel that others who have never struggled cannot understand or are constantly judging you, but when you are in the boat together, you can form a kind of family system where you encourage and reinforce the best about each other.

This means that the role of pastor is not just about helping the person break or redefine old relationships, but to help find new relationships. You are helping them to play a new role in a new system with healthy people. The first healthy person you are helping them relate to is you.

Reflection Questions

1. What are the two fundamental human needs?

2. Name some of the reasons why people do not experience the love of God.

3. Write your name on a sheet of paper. In a circle around your name, write the names of the people you are in closest relationship with and draw a line to the name. Now for each relationship, consider whether it is a healthy or unhealthy relationship. Does it bring you both joy or both pain?

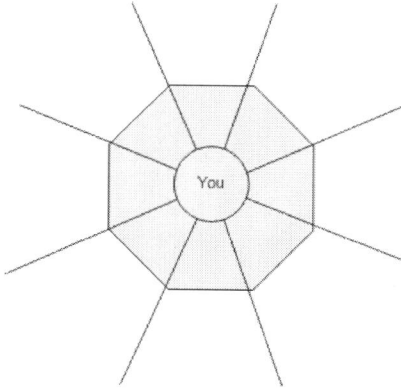

4. Repeat this exercise for someone you are pastoring or who is close to you.

Who You Are

Changing someone's relationship with God and their relationships with others ultimately changes who they are. This change in identity is the goal of pastoral ministry. It involves putting off the natural, Satanically-influenced and sinful identity and stepping into their God-given identity and potential. This means half of the process is putting off the earthly, and the other half is putting on the heavenly. The question we have all asked ourselves is: if the blood of Jesus is so powerful, why is it that no matter what theology we use, sin itself is so powerful?

LIFETRAPS

In the church, when someone has deep problems, we often say they have a "stronghold." The word "stronghold" puts focus in the wrong place, however. It makes us think in terms of demons victimizing us against our will. Actually, what keeps you in the life you are living is your own thoughts, actions, and experiences. It's not even the sin itself, it's the way of experiencing the world that drives the sin. It is the fundamental emotional operating system at the core of your identity. This operating system starts being formed at the earliest ages, and is continually reinforced as you grow older.

Because every person is born separated from God and can only progressively come into relationship with God as they are born again, they find other ways to meet their emotional needs. This leads to the person becoming wired in a certain way, into a certain pattern of sin that repeats. This is what some secular counselors have called a "lifetrap." Since relationships and experiences are what shape your identity, lifetraps are just a way of talking about what your identity actually contains.

The developer of schema therapy, Dr. Jeff Young, identifies 11 major kinds of lifetraps. There may be others, but this list, developed from extensive professional experience, is a very good starting place to consider the key ways people get stuck:

Lifetrap	Dominant Thought
Abandonment	"Please don't leave me!"
Emotional Deprivation	"I'll never get the love I need."
Mistrust and Abuse	"I can't trust you."
Social Exclusion	"I don't fit in."
Dependence	"I can't make it on my own."
Fear	"Catastrophe is about to strike:"
Defectiveness	"I'm worthless."
Failure	"I feel like such a failure."
Subjugation	"I always do it your way."
Unrelenting Standards	"It's never quite good enough."
Entitlement	"I can have whatever I want."

Remember, this is not a list of problems. This is a list of the problems *behind* other problems. Your surface problem might be a pornography addiction, but the problem behind that is that you feel worthless all the time and pornography makes you feel better. Lifetraps are emotional worldviews. They are ways you process information that the world sends you.

Think about it this way: when you have a lifetrap, you run everything that happens to you through that lifetrap filter. For example, if you have a fear problem, then you judge experiences by how safe they make you feel, and you do things to prevent yourself from feeling out of control. It is a script which runs behind everything else, and a place that you go to meet your needs. Or if you have emotional deprivation, you judge every relationship by whether or not it is filling your deep emotional needs. And you try everything in your power to make them do so. These patterns become a deep part of your identity. It usually takes time to rewrite these programs and get into the heart of God instead.

This is important to understand because getting free means focusing in the right place with the right expectations. We always have to look deeper than we are accustomed to looking. A person's primary problem is not a demon. The person may have a demon that needs to be cast out, and if the opportunity arises, you should cast it out. But even then, the reason the demon was there in the first place was due to the lifetrap – the pattern of sinful thinking and emotional responses.

Lifetraps create a system of emotional rewards and punishments. For example, Stan has a problem where he disconnects from other and rarely responds to their calls or text messages. Even though in his heart he wants these relationships, he never behaves in the way that would create those close connections. The questions is, why? Is it possible for him to simply start responding to text messages? Well, he could force himself but it would only work for a while. More fundamentally there is a set of emotional rewards and punishments taking place. A healthy person feels positive about human contact and naturally wants to respond to it. They are getting an emotional reward from the closeness created by relationship and so they want to do it naturally. Stan, however, doesn't experience this. When he gets a message it creates stress and pressure. This feeling of pressure makes it very negative for him to want to respond to a message even if he wants to, and so he rarely does.

Stan's lifetrap is unrelenting standards. He puts an extreme amount of pressure on himself to perform inside relationships, and this makes conducting relationships very burdensome. Stan will be unable to change his relationships until this fundamental structure in his heart is changed. His lifetrap has created a situation where relationships are punished and isolation is rewarded, and that drives his behavior. When he receives ministry to change his identity in this core area, then he will find himself wanting to relate to and connect with others.

The deficits described the lifetrap also describes what a person's idol will be. If you don't put God into the void in your life, you will put something else in, and that is the idol. Idols can be all kinds of things, from relationships to success, cars, self-image, to "upside-down idols" like pride in your own dysfunction. The point is, however, that an idol is something you cling to, to deal with life because you believe it is meeting your needs. If you have the worthlessness lifetrap, you might cling to all kinds of things that you do to make yourself look important or valuable. An idol is usually marked by something that a person refuses to give up.

They might even place an emotional perimeter around it so that you feel you cannot even address that area.

Because people cling so tightly to their idols, it can be counter-productive to confront them head on. Sometimes an idol does need to be confronted directly, but more often, I try to minster to the reason why the idol is there in the first place. This is the lifetrap. If I start to attack why you feel worthless, addressing the unhealthy ways you are trying to meet your need for self-worth will be much easier. If I come directly against your obvious problem, your gut reaction will be to defend yourself and your idol.

THREE AREAS OF MINISTRY

There are three main areas where ministry needs to be applied to bring freedom: actions, thoughts, and emotions. The most obvious and visible part of sin is the action. Stopping outward behaviors is an important first step to freedom. This is because the more you sin, the more you want to sin, and the more your brain is wired to sin. As an example, recent research into the effect of pornography on a man's mind has made this especially clear. When a man goes to meet his emotional needs through pornography, his brain gets rewired in a way that makes it hard for him to have real human relationships. It makes him desire the false relationship with pornography even more. Some men with severe problems in this area cannot even become excited by a real woman. Sin has rewired their brain. Therefore, cutting off the pattern of sin is essential to freedom. The brain actually has to rewire to cherish real women and see them as more than a sex symbol. We do not pretend that stopping the outward sin is freedom, but it is an important step. You can't clean up the house when the sewer is still running into it. Once the sewer is shut off, then cleanup can begin.

The second part of sin is the beliefs and thoughts which lead to the bad behavior. These false beliefs make the sin look desirable and drive you to repeat it. One of the pastor's roles is to help the person identify what these false beliefs are and develop ways to address them. This is an area where the church has spent a lot of energy. Most of us know something about "taking every thought captive" and redeeming our minds to the thought process of the Bible. This is good.

This brings us to the third component to sin: emotions. Thoughts are very important and they must be taken captive, but thoughts emerge as a response to emotional needs. If your mother never shows you love, you just feel bad for a long time. Only later do you begin to put words on it or consciously think, "My mother doesn't love me." Changing this thought would be helpful but doing this alone will not fix everything, especially if the thought is really true and your mom really did reject you. You have to find a whole new emotional stream that will prevent you from feeling pain or numbness whenever the topic comes up or you're around your mom. The only way to do this is to have an actual encounter with God. Experiencing God, and then beginning healing relationships with others, will come and fill in these emotional gaps.

I have known and worked with many people throughout my pastoral ministry—from those who are barely motivated, to those who are absolutely on fire for God. And the one thing I can say for sure is that real transformation takes *time*. Think about how long it took to establish a lifetrap in the first place. By the time you encounter someone coming for counseling, it has usually been in place for decades. In the spirit-filled church, our belief in God's miracle working power sometimes causes us to assume that all of our problems should be fixed instantly at the altar. That would be the equivalent of getting a completely different personality instantaneously. If this actually happened, people would literally not know who you were…you yourself would not know! And although some bondages can be broken instantaneously, the real legwork is always long term. God took decades to make Abraham the father of faith, He took 40 years in the desert to prepare Moses as the deliverer, and took 3 ½ years to Himself pastor twelve hand-picked men to their calling.

The kind of transformation we are seeking therefore takes not just one, but many miraculous encounters with God over the long term. In the case of someone I worked with who has developed a very successful ministry, and was absolutely on fire at the start, and open to correction, it took about five years to deal with the fundamental issues blocking his calling. During this process he had several very dramatic encounters with God, addressed very challenging relationship problems with others, and spent lots of time in prayer. This gives you a realistic picture of what a life transformation looks like. It is a long term process of helping someone to walk with God and break the patterns that have kept them where they are. True pastoral care is helping someone rewire their identity to be based in God. And any true freedom that comes must address all three parts—their actions, thoughts and emotions.

THE EMOTIONAL THREAD

Perhaps the least understood part of this trio is the emotional realm. Changing actions or thoughts seems straightforward enough, but how can you address someone's emotions? The process of bringing someone to freedom is nothing less than rewriting part of their identity. Since this identity was shaped formed through a series of experiences, part of addressing them is also experiential. It involves a combination of healing past experiences as well as having new healthy ones. The goal is to help the person make new emotional connections.

One way that many ministers have tried to address this need is through Theophostic prayer. In Theophostic prayer, the person is encouraged to revisit past memories and ask God to speak to them about the situation. The idea is that all bondages have their ultimate root in childhood experiences, and that repairing these experiences leads to freedom. Theophostic prayer has helped many people, but rather than consider it *the* fundamental way that people are helped, we consider it to be a tool in identity transformation which is only used as needed. The truth is, we don't need to go digging to find something in the past for every issue that comes up, nor should we look at ourselves as victims of circumstance or upbringing.

I prefer to think instead in terms of fixing an "emotional thread." The emotional thread is the set of life experiences, related feelings, and current attitudes that shape a person's interactions. Addressing this emotional thread has a past and present component. A friend of mine learned that he had difficulty receiving love. This difficulty was related to the fact that his mother's love for him always came in the form of pushing him to do things. He didn't have many warm bonding experiences with his mom so he never developed a sense of being comfortable with himself. They had a very positive relationship so he didn't need to revisit a bunch of wounds or pain, and in fact did not realize until recently that there was any connection from past to present. It was not his mother's fault that he has difficulty receiving love, but the way the relationship played out led to a void in this area. Therefore ministering to this relationship is a way to help put Humpty Dumpty back together again.

This relationship could receive ministry in a variety of ways. First there is an opportunity to go back to his mother and seek some aspect of what he didn't get because they have a positive relationship. He could open up a dialog with his mother which might help him understand or receive better love from her. Although he can never be a child again, and his mother is unlikely to totally change, God might even orchestrate a moment at the present where he could get some piece of what it is he did not receive as a child.

Secondly, this man, because he is married but had a bonding gap with his own mother, is lacking the emotional skills to bond properly with his wife. He can't feel the connection he longs to feel. A way of addressing this emotional thread that has run throughout his life is to begin to change the dynamics of the relationship with his wife. If he continues to do things in the relationship that make him hard to bond to, she will never give him the kind of comfort she is capable of giving—and the emotional thread will strengthen. If he changes the relationship with her, however, she will also change how she responds to him and he can get a portion of what he is lacking emotionally. The emotional thread will change and begin to rewire.

Third, there may be an aspect of Theophostic prayer which is helpful. This man had memories of the past where he sought comfort from his mother but received something else. Through prayer, God can both heal the pain of such situations and work on the heart level beliefs associated with them—the negative scripts. By addressing each one of them, and turning away from the painful beliefs associated with it, God can rewrite this part of his identity.

What's important about all of these approaches is that they do not place blame on someone else. Blame does not lead to freedom, but only to more bondage. This man is taking responsibility for his own beliefs and relationships and inviting God to help change them. It's not about telling his mother, "You didn't do this for me!" Or hounding his wife, "Why don't you comfort me?" It

35

is about him understanding that he has a deficit which hurts his relationships. His actions should be oriented towards changing his relationships to address that deficit. They are not silver bullets. They are ways of partnering with God to rewire his emotions. Over time God will help him fill in the gaps.

When you minister to someone, you will be ministering to their relationship with God, their relationships with others, and their fundamental emotional operating system or lifetraps. As you address each of these components, you will progressively see change in the person.

NEW IDENTITY

The fact is, however, you can never dig deep enough into sin to get rid of it. The digging process is helpful for putting off the earthly nature, but if it becomes the overriding focus, your success stops at the door of self-help. For pastoral care to be truly successful, you must step out of sinful thoughts and patterns *and into God*. Understanding sin is only helpful to the degree that it helps you step out of yourself and into Him. It's natural for pastoral care and counseling to become about problems and sin, but that will only keep people down if it's the only part. A huge part of people growing in Christ is seeing themselves as He sees them, fixing their eyes on Him, on His love for them on His dreams for them, the exciting things He has for them. This means that although dealing with problems and sin are fundamental to anyone's growth, the pastoral relationship shouldn't always be about the bad things that people have, but about the good things they should have.

Take Warren. The world would say he is an "alcoholic." This is a powerful label which defines him. He is always wrestling with "not being an alcoholic." When he meets people or sits down together with me, that's the natural discussion. "How do I quit drinking?" or, "Why do I drink?" These kinds of questions put all of the focus on the sin. Although they are important and must be explored and discussed, that can't be the framework by which you see the entire process. Warren will find it impossible to "not" be something. Instead he needs to "be" something. He needs truth spoken over his life. Just as Satan has planted a false identity as an "alcoholic" in his life, God has a true identity which He wants to call out of Warren. There are dreams and visions that God has placed inside of Warren that He wants to draw him into.

Part of what you do as pastor is speak to those things. You begin show him what his place and value in the body are. You begin to show him his unlimited potential, and help him to see himself not as an alcoholic or something struggling sin, but as a child of God with a purpose possibility to accomplish things in his life. Ministering the truth to someone in this way makes sin obsolete. Instead of "to sin or not to sin," it is "to be who God has made me or not." Do you see how it reverses the discussion? It puts Warren's focus on God instead of on sin, and that itself is one of the most important elements of defeating sin.

The more a person grows and begins to see themselves in this light, the more that pastoral care becomes about pursuing God instead of fighting sin. You become the coach who helps facilitate the hunger of God in their life and remove obstacles, instead of the doctor who is always trying to save them from an emergency.

Reflection Questions

1. Take a look at the Lifetrap chart. Do any of these statements stand out to you? Have they made themselves into your operating script? What kinds of regular behaviors or attitudes do they drive in you?

2. Take at least one sinful behavior you have and trace it back through its outward signs, the thoughts you have which cause it, and the feelings you have that propel the thoughts. Can you see any patterns? Does it relate to a lifetrap?

3. How long do you expect it to take, realistically, to rid yourself of this sin, if you diligently pursued it in God? What things from God, and what things from others, would be required to get complete victory? What kind of regular accountability or action plan would you need?

4. This process is what you will be taking others through, who may not want freedom as much as you or have the capabilities in God that you do. They may also have more sins and entanglements. How does this adjust your expectations for what is required, how long it will take, and what your role is? Will you make any changes in your approach?

Part II – The Counseling Process

Connection

Confession

Ministry

Action

Making a Connection

The counseling process moves through several stages: connection, confession, ministry, and action. When you meet someone right off, the first goal is to make a connection. You need to establish trust and rapport. They need to feel like you are a safe person, a person that loves them, a person that can understand what they are experiencing, and a person who actually has some wisdom that might help them out. You might be counseling a friend or someone referred to you that you've never met before. Either way you have to develop the relationship so that as you understand their needs, they trust you and open up to you. Sometimes if they are a trusting person or you are from similar backgrounds, this can happen in a single meeting. But sometimes it might take a couple of meetings just to get the person to relax a bit. Either way, connection is the first step, before which nothing significant can really happen.

CONNECTION: FORMING A PASTORAL RELATIONSHIP

If someone goes for counseling to the pastor of their church or a professional counselor, the counselor has the benefit of automatic professional authority. The counselee is going explicitly because they have a problem and are looking for an authoritative answer. The counselor will talk for a while, ask some questions, and then give advice that will be trusted by virtue of their professional position, not because of any relationship. They are fulfilling a professional rather than a personal role.

The kind of pastoral care we are talking about however, is rarely like this, however. It often begins because someone around you has a need and you are in a position to give helpful advice. Until you become fairly advanced, people will not be referred to you or trust you because of your reputation. And in fact, by the time someone reaches out for that level of help, they are usually in a position of real desperation. What we want to happen is something much more organic and basic. We want people to form pastoral relationships in real life which will lead to their growth. This means they will get help before they reach crisis point. But how does that happen?

It happens through a normal personal relationship where you build trust and authority over time. As you build relationship, the person will trust you more to unlock the mysteries of their life. They will see that you have the wisdom they need to help them move to the next place. The pastoral caregiver is like the "friend who sticks closer than a brother" (Proverbs 18:24). You walk alongside a person and model the love of Christ to them. You are not simply telling them about it, you are demonstrating it in the context of your relationship. You are a friend who provides wisdom, who helps the person see what is going on in their heart without judgment.

Because this relationship is built on trust, it cannot be forced. In my early days of ministry, I was so eager to help people and so intuitively aware of their needs, that I would dive right in. People would engage me, but usually it blew up in my face. I had started to pastor them without them wanting to be pastored. You must recognize that not everyone who has a problem is ready to work on it. Ad not everyone who is ready to work on it is going to be a good fit for you personally. Even if you had all of the wisdom needed to unlock their problems, they still must be ready to face them and respect you enough to want your input specifically.

This respect may come from your age, your ministry experiences, your life experiences, or in some cases by them receiving form your ministry in some other way – such as through prayer, preaching, or conversation. Regardless of where it comes from, nothing can proceed without it. Do not simply jump in and start trying to fix people. Start with a normal friendship and wait and see if they begin to open up to you. This means paying attention, listening, and showing interest in them as a human being. It means showing that you can relate in some important way to who they are and their life situation. This is especially true if they are going through something really difficult. No one wants advice from a know-it-all who had never faced any adversity.

Therefore an important part of forming a connection is often being real with people about your deepest difficulties and your personal story. What have you overcome? What challenges have you faced? Don't tell them how amazing you are. Let them see the parts of your life that aren't amazing. For most people, this is very disarming. They will begin to trust you by virtue of your transparency and honesty.

For me personally, this means I often share the story of almost being killed in a car accident and all of the associated trauma. I may share some aspect of my walk with God, such as the phase of my life where I dealt with severe legalism and thought I would drop into the pit of hell, or the time I spent in a cult-like group. Sharing these kinds of difficult experiences create a natural connection. Instead of looking like a minister with all of the answers, I look like the regular guy that I actually am, with real life experiences.

In the same way, showing empathy is very important to establishing a connection with someone. If they share something difficult, they need to know that you feel the gravity of the situation they are in. You may have never experienced anything like it, but you need to resonate on the same emotional level they are at. When you show empathy, you are identifying with them in their situation, stepping in and being emotionally present in their reality. Look them in the eyes, say something that reflects that you "get it." Show emotional presence in their life.

If you are able to build a connection between the two of you and it is clear that they are open to input from you on their life, you are then in a position to form a pastoral relationship. Never move beyond this phase until it is clear that they are open to input, and that you have the kind of relationship which would allow them to receive it from you.

THE NATURE OF THE PASTORAL RELATIONSHIP

Although the pastoral relationship is rooted in friendship and trust, it is not the same as any average friendship. It is a friendship where you play the role of mentor and advisor. The price of this kind of input is that you take on special responsibilities. In a normal friendship, both people give and take a little bit, and learn how to be kind to one another to avoid negative emotions. They negotiate lots of compromises and tolerate each other in various ways. It has balance.

In a pastoral relationship, rather than negotiate a compromise, you as pastor absorb some of the emotional fallout. If your counselee has negative behaviors, rather than push back, you will need to overlook it until God opens the right moment to deal with it. In this way it is like the role of a parent. Children do all kinds of negative things, but a good parent never gets down on that level – instead they progressively lead the child to maturity so that they are prepared for healthy lifelong relationships. When you are walking alongside a person in that posture, especially a person who is less than healthy, but really anyone, you will experience them putting their negative emotions on you. This is *emotional displacement*. You are taking the emotional burdens that their other relationships have been unable to bear.

For example, consider a person with severe rejection issues. A person like this often has at least one of their parental relationships completely broken. A person like this also acts in ways that ensure they get more rejection. They might have awkward communication styles or say things at in appropriate times, etc. These behaviors will run off any "normal" person who just wants to be a normal friend. This means that the person experiences more and more rejection as they go. So they will do these things to you. They might even test you by doing things designed to make you reject them. They might, for example, run hot and cold. They will be extremely open, and move forward quickly for a while, and then later they will just shut down or disappear. This of course would be a hurtful behavior in a normal relationship. If you were the friend, you might simply just quit calling or coming over, but as the pastoral friend, you simply pick back up and continue to model love.

In a pastoral role you do not react by rejecting, leaving, or mocking the dysfunctional person. You act like the perfect "Christ-friend," who loves them in the midst of their dysfunction. By that I don't mean, "Wow, you're dysfunctional, but I love you anyway." I mean you overlook their behavior and continue to stay in a secure posture. This is a lot like what a parent does. When your child acts up, you do not reject them, you correct them and continue your posture of unconditional love. And as a parent, you might be selective about what you correct and when because the most important thing is that the child maintain that love connection to you regardless of what else might happen.

What a parent does is model a healthy relationship and help their child conform to that healthy relationship. If the parent gets self-pitying and has a childish argument, or mocks, or pouts in response to their child, then they are modeling an unhealthy relationship. The child will enter into life without the capacity for mature negotiation. But you, as the pastor, will encounter a lot of this behavior in your adult congregation! You'll find people who never had a healthy relationship where unconditional love was modeled and therefore have had to rely on various coping mechanisms. You are in some ways trying to participate with God as He "re-parents" the person. In that role you have to model unconditional love and show them how to better respond to their issues.

This is what I call the *relational surrogate*. You are modeling Christ by absorbing the emotional displacement, always returning love regardless of their behavior. What will happen over time as they have a healthy relationship with you, is they will begin to develop the capacities to have a healthier relationships with others and with God. You are their real-life model of God's love and interaction. They don't simply need to believe what you say about God or relationship with others, they need to experience it themselves through you.

This means that although the relationship centers around you helping them, it is not completely one-dimensional either. You may need to model various other dimensions of relationship. This can mean anything from watching a movie together, going to an event they are participating in, or simply going to the grocery store together. Just as Jesus was a real person who did normal things with the disciples, not simply a talking head, you are a real person as well. You are parachuting down into the middle of someone's life and showing them love in the ways that matter to them.

Although there is a parental dimension to all of this, it doesn't you are actually "over" the person to the extent a parent is. This will lead to all kinds of unhealthy dynamics. Since you are dealing with an adult, you are more in the posture of an older brother, or a coach. You are the friend who loves all the time, who knows things, and who helps them stop sabotaging their life.

None of this means that you do not address their behavior. In fact, that's a key part of what you are doing in this role — progressively addressing their various dysfunctional behaviors. But you need to do so in "priority order." Unlike a normal person who might just run away, or get annoyed, you look past behaviors on the surface, while you try to gain access and address the deepest aspects of a person's life. For example, one person that I pastor called me a few months ago and started yelling and swearing. He was under a lot of stress and angry with God. Under more normal circumstances, I might have corrected him or shut it down. But in this case, that would have only served to alienate him and cut off access to deal with the roots of why he was really angry. I listened, told him that I loved him, and a few days later we returned to deal with those deeper issues. As a pastor, you can't just fire off and start correcting everything a person does. You work on one item with them and wink at the others.

In fact, sometimes issues on the surface will be the points by which you can gain access to the deeper issues. One person I pastored had a habit of disappearing for long stretches. I overlooked it for a while until I got the right moment. Then when I asked about it in a non-threatening way it lead to the revelation that he was afraid of emotionally burdening me – and everyone else – when he was having trouble. This got me access to the real pastoral issue.

And instead of giving talking-head advice to him, we had a real living relationship so I was able to give real feedback about how he is not a burden at all and how I look forward to hearing from him. These kinds of moments give you the opportunity to reinforce your love for someone. As you reinforce your love, you are demonstrating to them what it's like to really be loved by God. You are helping their heart learn a new behavior. Whoever was in their life before was easily run off by their strange behavior, but you aren't. You are modeling God's relentless and constant love. By playing that role, you help them to really grasp God's love and release the dysfunctional behavior.

Having these kinds of interactions over and over again, of course, can be painful. If you were just a talking head, there would be nothing personal about it, but you are actually in a relationship with the person. If they stand you up, it hurts; if they swear at you it hurts. When they run away from you, it hurts. When they shut you down, it hurts. When they reject specifically because you loved them, it hurts even more. This is the emotional displacement. It's the pain caused by loving someone in real life, and not hitting back. Loving someone who is function and loves you back (like your spouse) of course has ups and downs and moments of pain, but loving someone who is less functional and less able to appreciate and reciprocate your love is challenging. I have found, however, that feeling this pain helps you really understand God's love at a whole different level since this is exactly how God loves us all the time. He loves when you ignore Him, and He keeps on loving, seeking, forgiving you, and always being nice regardless of what you do. In response, we run, reject, and do all kinds of dysfunctional things. Of course if you don't "get down into the trenches" with your people you can avoid the pain, and just dole out advice, but I just don't see God that way. He came down to earth into the middle of our lives and experiences it with us.

This does not mean that you simply put up with anything and everything or allow yourself to be abused. It means that you look at the relationship through the perspective of their good, not your own. You address relationship issues because they need it, not because you are frustrated. The bond you form by loving them this way is the conduit through which the healing flows. You form a bond with the person and show them love through their seasons, which helps them deal with the roots of the behavior as well as changing the behavior itself.

Reflection Questions

1. Have you ever forced pastoring on someone who didn't want it? Or didn't respect you as a pastoral figure? How did this end up?

2. What kinds of unique adversities have you had which you could build on, as a counselor? What kinds of situations provoke empathy for you naturally, and which are harder?

3. Can you handle someone "shooting the messenger" or putting their negative emotions on you? What kinds of negative behaviors might you have to overlook more in your pastoral relationships? Are any of these particularly difficult?

4. Consider one person you are working with right now and prioritize their issues. What are the main roots that have to be dealt with? What sabotaging behaviors need to be dealt with along the way, to get to those roots? What unhealthy behaviors are farther down the line?

5. Most pastors need a way to decompress after a heavy conversation with a difficult person. Do you have a good coping mechanism? A safe person who can handle any fallout negative emotions you have?

Confession

Once you have established trust, you need to get the real problem to the surface. This may happen very quickly because their situation is urgent or because you hit it off well. Or it may take some time. Regardless, the goal is for the person to "spill." Locked up inside the person's heart are all of their real problems, and your goal is to help get these to the surface.

I like to use the analogy of a splinter. When you get a splinter in your hand, it causes a great degree of pain. If you do not remove it, your skin will naturally try to cover it, but until the splinter is removed it will always be a source of pain. If a splinter is deep, it may take some significant effort to remove it. You may have to cut a bit, and there is a good chance it will hurt. But the moment the splinter is pulled, the real healing begins. This is exactly what you are doing in pastoral counseling. You are uncovering the splinter and pulling back layers of skin so that the real problem can be exposed and dealt with. This is the *confession* phase.

You are the facilitator of this process. You need to explore together with them, in the presence of the Holy Spirit, exactly what is going on. Ask questions until you have a grasp of what is causing the problem. Sometimes the person may have an idea of what is causing their problem, but sometimes they have no idea at all. Sometimes they are even wrong about what their problem is. Do not assume that whatever they say is bothering them is actually the root problem. They may just be explaining a symptom to you, and often times the way they are seeing the problem is itself a big part of the problem. It takes some dialogue to figure out the root cause. By asking lots of questions and exploring the issue, you begin to develop a sense of what is really going on in their life. You want to get below the surface, explore their history, and just keep going until you have full picture of their situation. This requires good questions and good listening.

THE LISTENING POSTURE

I used to think that I could change people just by talking to them. If I gave them the advice they needed to hear, they would receive it, take action, and everything would be fine. But the more that I have worked with people, the more I have learned that the exact opposite is mostly true: what the person hears is what matters, not what I say. Information itself does not solve problems. Often the information or guidance a person needs has already been given to them by someone else, or is otherwise readily available. Something else is causing them to stay stuck.

People change when truth finally gets into their heart. But how does that happen? It is a process, and it is voluntary, which means they have to give themselves permission to consider something different than what they already believe. They must be open to change. Direct confrontation with truth often just leads people to confirm their rejection of the truth. It is only as a person lets down their guard and becomes hungry for the truth, and open to receiving it from you, that what you say will make any difference. What this means is that you need to walk through a process to help them open up. As they open up and confess their situation, you gain access to help shape their perceptions by the questions you ask and the way you reflect their own statements back to them.

The first part of listening is getting the other person to talk. As they talk you must resist the urge to dole out answers and advice throughout the entire process. You are partnering with God to bring forward the things of the heart so that the person themselves can become aware of it. If you jump in right away with answers, you will shut down the flow of communication and block their thought process. It is about them and God, not you and them.

This kind of talking is revelatory. As you create a safe atmosphere, and help them explore what is going on, they will be able to access deep realms of their heart which they might otherwise block. Jesus explains in Matthew 12:34 that it is "out of the abundance of a man's heart he speaks." When someone begins to talk, they reveal much more than what they say, they reveal the condition of their heart, something about who they are, and how they relate to God.

Maintain a warm posture pretty much regardless of what they say. This helps cultivate a sense of comfort and closeness between you. The more "air time" another person gets in a conversation, the more understood they feel. To some extent, it doesn't even matter if you don't completely understand. They feel connected to you because you are listening. You have heard them and haven't judged, condemned, or corrected them. You are giving them space to develop and explore who they are. Interject into the conversation in ways that will make them feel like you are their friend and you can relate to their feelings. Draw on a story from your own life which connects with their story so they know you have something in common, that you fundamentally like them, and are trustworthy. If they do not feel like you relate to them, are trustworthy, or you love them, nothing else is going to matter.

Although you are there as pastor to help decode the mysteries of their lives, recognize that this only happens by permission. You have to resist the temptation to enter into any relationship with the presumption that you are the wise one. After you have helped enough people you may feel like you have skills and answers, but the fact is that every person and situation is unique. If you come in with the attitude that you have the answers, people will sense that and shut down. You are not coming in as one who is *over* them, you are coming in as one who is *with* them.

First, they need to sense that you are their friend. A friend who is there with them and can help them find answers. You are not there to substitute for God, you are there as a partner to help them hear and obey God. You cannot control what the other person is going to do, nor should you try. It will simply make both of you frustrated and abort the process. You are responsible to God for the quality of guidance and care you give, not for what the other person does with that guidance. You are the coach, but coaches don't get to carry the football. All they can do is help you train and call the right plays.

This doesn't mean that you listen with a neutral ear as though you have no answers to give. Unlike secular counseling, the goal of pastoral listening is not to get your counselee to find their "own" answers, but to get them to hear God. That is what you're doing as you listen too. You are listening to God while they talk. You are listening for Him to reveal certain things about the person to you, to highlight what is important and give you ideas on where to go with the discussion. This is where the Holy Spirit comes in. Listening with a spiritual ear is a difficult art to learn, but I cannot overemphasize how important it is to the entire counseling process. The human tendency is to be either overinvolved and controlling, or under-involved and irrelevant

Think of yourself instead as a collaborator. You are neither there to solve their problems, nor just to watch. You are getting involved in their world. This takes pressure off of you and the relationship. If you are in control of the relationship, they will do exactly what you say, then be upset with you when it doesn't work, and then reject the truths you gave them. The first time they fail, the relationship will likely be over. When you are a collaborator, however, the relationship has room for both of you to be human. There is room for them to disagree with your input and see where that takes them. Usually this means that it is an area where they are not yet ready to hear the truth, and that's ok. Rather than force it on them, it is usually best just to step back and let them walk that decision out for themselves. You will be there to help them interpret the results, and that will help them be more open to the truth the next time.

The fact is, that even if you become extremely skilled in counseling, you will never have all the answers. God is the one who searches the heart and guides the direction of a man's life. You may sometimes give wrong advice, wrongly timed advice, or advice that will be misheard. The relationship needs room for this to happen. Remember, your goal is to plug them into the Source, not be the source.

QUESTIONS

Part of listening is the art of asking questions. This is what Jesus demonstrates in Mark 8:29 when he asks Peter, "Who do you say that I am?" Peter had just given a little speech about what others thought, but Jesus was trying to draw out of Peter what *he* thought. Jesus already knew what Peter thought, and He certainly didn't have ego needs—He asked because he wanted to draw the truth out of Peter. This is exactly what the good pastor does over and over again. You want to draw out what people actually believe deep inside. You want them to confess and name their own problems, and you want to help them discover the solutions.

Some amount of asking questions requires "mining." The first thing someone says is usually a surface perspective of a situation. It might be a standard religious answer they know they are supposed to give, or they might have said it because that's what they always say. They might not feel safe enough to tell you the deeper reality, or they might not know it. That's why you build trust and make them feel safe. Taking over the conversation makes it hard for someone to hit the most sensitive areas on their heart, but the more you listen and love while you listen, the more safe they will feel to get to the deeper, harder truth. But you also must "mine," meaning drill deep beyond the surface. If they themselves had already really understood their issue, they would not have the issue in the first place. You are asking questions to try to get to a mutual discovery about what is going on. It's a puzzle where you dive deeper and deeper until you are both clear about what the real issue is.

In this deeper discovery phase of listening, you are helping to develop a model which explains both to you and to them what they are feeling. Take this simple line of questions as an example:

"Why did you do that?"

"Because I was scared"

"Scared of what?"

"Being alone."

"Have you been alone a lot in your life?"

"My mother left me alone all the time"

In this exchange the counselor is diving underneath to try to find out what is really going on in the person's head. He needs to know what experiences, feelings, and beliefs are causing the counselee to feel a certain way. This is not a cross-examination or "guru" discussion. It's a process of mutual discovery. You are asking questions to help them figure it out. The questions are leading questions, however, they aren't just open ended. You might repeat these questions, but you still never know where it is going. Jesus has the answers. The Holy Spirit will reveal things through the conversation. The questions follow His leading to the root cause of the issue. It's like a trail of breadcrumbs.

Once you have gotten to the root or core issue, sometimes that is a good place to pause. One of the things you need to do is say back to the person what they have told you. Here are a couple of examples of how you might phrase that:

"So you have these feelings of loneliness whenever you are in a crisis?"

"So there is a lot of pain there in your relationship with your mom?"

By doing this you help the person hear their own heart. Just because a person is speaking does not mean that they are really listening or aware of what they are saying. When you say things back to them, you help them to hear themselves.

Remember, this is a partnership. They have a say, too. One of the biggest mistakes pastoral counselors make is to force a model on someone. You may feel that you know exactly what their problem is, but if you force it on them, it may not fit exactly. Think of it like your mom making you wear an awkward sweater to school. She might think it is perfect, but if you don't identify with it, it can be a very negative experience for you and shut down the relationship. The starting point must always be the person's self-understanding of the problem. For example, let's say you think a person is struggling with insecurity. You ask them if the problem feels like insecurity, but after honest reflection, they do not resonate with it. Don't push it, but explore a different avenue. On the other hand, if the person does not receive *any* of your ideas or models, or if they always have to twist them around, then it is also not a collaboration. You are wasting your time and they will exhaust you. The goal is for you to be working together, trying on different sweaters until you find the one that fits.

PASTOR AS INTERPRETER

This process of drawing out the deep things of someone's heart through listening is at the core of helping someone grow. I consider it the most fundamental skill you need to pastor someone. After listening comes the next important skill of interpreting. Listening is the door to unlocking the heart, but once it is open, you must help your person give definition to what is inside, so they can gain power over it.

When someone hears and recognizes their own problem, it gives them something to work with. God may have tried many times to highlight their problem to them before, and it may be floating around in the back of their mind, but when you bring it forward and say it back, this gives it true definition – a name. That's a huge part of the role of the pastor in a counseling encounter: to help the person name and give correct definition to the problem they are facing. Once their enemy has a name, they can start to conquer it instead of chasing the wind.

Personal problems need names and definitions because emotions are not naturally and easily understood. You learn to understand them by others naming them for you as they see your behavior. This started when you are little. When you were a baby and you cried, your mom said to you things like, "Oh, are you sad?" And when you laughed, she said, "Oh, you're so happy!" When she did this, she was helping you develop an emotional vocabulary. Today your friends and family do the same thing when they say you look angry or seem depressed. Really understanding what is going on in your heart and what to do about it is a skill learned over a lifetime.

This is especially true for those who missed those key developmental moments as children. What if your mom never asked you if you were sad or happy? What if she never displayed any emotions? What if your dad never told you he loved you? What if your parents mocked you when you showed fear or vulnerability? When you fail to form a bond or develop an emotional vocabulary, a variety other unhealthy things happen. A person may:

- Shut down all emotional information and become laconic, completely unaware of their own emotions.

- Become significantly introverted, phobic, or resentful of human attachments. They may live alone and reject outreach.

- Experience love as pain, and pain as love. When someone is warm to you it hurts, and when someone hurts you it makes you feel loved. This naturally happens for those who have been abused in some way.

- Become emotionally manipulative, narcissistic, or in the worst case sociopathic. They learn to understand emotions, but they only use them to gain power over others. This person never feels a true bond with anyone else.

These kinds of issues require significant long term care to unravel. In severe cases, they are almost impossible to reverse. In more moderate cases, you continue to socialize with people normally but stay disconnected from your deepest emotions. You spend more time maintaining appearances than being real. Most relationships in the world have some element of this dynamic, so it is very common to encounter people who have gotten saved but are not really in touch with their emotions or real motivations because everything has been on the surface.

Part of the pastor's role then, is as an emotional interpreter. Just like mom asked you, "Are you sad?" when you cried as a baby, the pastor asks and helps discern at a more complex level: "Do you think you are lashing out because you feel insecure?" Just by asking a question like this you are giving people a vocabulary by which to understand their problem. Then they can respond, "Actually, you know I think it might be more that I'm afraid of looking stupid." As they confess things from the heart, you float different ideas past them of what it might be and see how it resonates. This is an exploratory process. It's like exploratory surgery. They say some things and you ask questions. As you ask questions, you experience the Holy Spirit helping to direct the conversation. You float some more ideas and ask more targeted questions. The two of you are cooperatively listening to God to help get to the root of the issue:

"I've noticed that you cut me off a lot. I wonder why you do that?"

"I don't know. I've never noticed."

"Is it because you're anxious?"

"Hmm. I felt condemned when you asked that last question."

"Ok, that's good. Let's talk about why you felt condemned."

You see? It's exploratory. You don't know where it is going, or what you are going to find. You are floating ideas and looking for what is going to stick. You are challenging simple answers to try to get to the reason behind the reason. If you can get to the reason why they feel condemned, then you are really dealing with something much more significant than their tendency to interrupt.

During the entire process you must maintain a neutral, non-judging, exploratory posture. It's important to ask diplomatic questions that keep the person feeling like you are a partner, not an accuser. That might be hard for some people and you might need to build trust to the place where they will feel loved rather than accused. But the point is, it's an exploratory, non-judging line of questions designed for both of you to get to emotional root causes.

At first, this all may be a little difficult, but after you have done this enough times with enough people, you start to see patterns and become good at it. Situations become familiar. You become comfortable with the basic mechanisms of the heart and are able to pull a lot from a little in order to move the ball forward more quickly.

This is why one of the things that you need in order to be an effective pastor is to have been pastored yourself. As you discover your own emotions, you are able to reflect against someone else's emotions. As someone helps you understand and identify your emotional motivations, you develop the skills to reflect on emotions in general, and see them in others. This is one of the most basic ways you discover what to say to someone. As they explain what they are feeling, bounce that off against your own emotions and experiences. How does what they are saying differ from what you would or do feel in the same situation? By comparing and contrasting you gain clues to what is broken in the person's emotional world.

This process of interpreting emotions is developmental. Some people may never have felt safe enough to express or put words on any of their emotions. In these cases, you will be starting at ground zero. You will have to provide most of the words. Make guesses of how they appear or seem to be feeling about something. Ask, "Does that make you feel [X]?" You are helping them understand and master their emotional world. You are helping them give names to patterns which hold them back. By giving it a name, and identifying a cause, you give them a place to fight. You give them the first piece of power over the situation.

HONESTY

With the average person, the listening process goes smoothly, but sometimes, you will encounter a smokescreen. The person is covering up their inner difficulties. They may be masking, even from themselves, what the real root cause is behind their behavior or statements. In some more challenging cases, they may not really have developed the capacity to be honest with themselves and discern what is going on. They have given false names and patterns to what is going on and you have to break through the smoke screen. For example, "I have a gift of discernment" may really mean, "I judge people because I need to feel superior to others." In these cases you will need to challenge self-lies to bring the truth into the picture. The truth can hurt, but the truth also is what sets people free. Nothing helps someone until they become emotionally honest about what is really going on.

One of the most common smokescreens I encounter in counseling are "in Christ" doctrines. A person will not want to explore or deal with deeper realities in their heart because they are "free in Christ" or a "new creation in Christ." These people are often some of the worst off and farthest from God because their doctrine gives them a feeling of being close to God without having to deal with their sins. When you try to hold the mirror up about where they really are, they repeat their theology instead of being honest. Rather than deal with the deeper issues, the person simply wants to skip ahead and declare they are wonderful. They might say, "I'm blessed and highly favored!" even though their life is falling completely apart. What needs to happen is for this person to get honest, and then let Christ address the fallout. As a person turns away from sinful thoughts and emotions, and towards Christ, they experience the true reality of their identity in Christ which is in desperate need of His love and mercy.

Confession is the process of exposing or getting at what the real problem is. In the average case, this is simply a process of making the person feel comfortable and heard. As you listen and ask questions with the help of the Holy Spirit, they will reveal the secrets of their heart. In the more advanced cases, you will need to progressively help the person develop emotional vocabulary and become comfortable with experiencing their emotions which may be new for them. And in the most difficult cases of all, you will need to confront the person's self-lies in order for them to have a real encounter with God.

The goal in any single session is not to solve or reveal every-thing. It is just to get a handle on something concrete that can be addressed. After you minister to that, you will repeat the process later and discover more.

Reflection Questions

1. When you counsel someone, do you do most of the talking or do they? Do you ever find yourself getting tired of giving people all the answers that they never act on?

2. Know your style: Have you ever had to abort the counseling process with someone because you were trying to "carry the football" for them? Why did you feel you had to? Or conversely, have you ever aborted the counseling process because you were too passive? You just listened to someone gripe all the time and didn't confront them with truth when you needed to?

3. Ask someone you trust how they feel when they share their emotions with you. Ask if there are any areas where they feel "unsafe" to share their feelings, and why.

4. Practice listening, asking questions, and interpreting with a friend or family member who needs it. Focus on letting them be heard and asking the Holy Spirit for guidance as you go.

5. What is your personal experience with being pastored? Could you hear another's counsel and accept it, or was it a negative experience for some reason? How will that affect your own counseling?

Ministry

Once you have a real issue on the table, then you can minister to it. Very often while the person is confessing, it will lead to a moment where it is clear that the Holy Spirit wants to minister to the person. There are really two kinds of ministry you will do: the ministry of truth, and the ministry of prayer. The ministry of truth is when you are helping them to see a new perspective on their situation. It is not completely separate and distinct from the listening process; it is something that is interwoven. As you are listening, they may say things which you know need to be addressed, and you must then look for the opportunity to give them truth. The ministry of prayer is when you turn to the Holy Spirit to do the work directly. The two work in concert together.

STORIES AND ANALOGIES

The truth is not as easy to communicate as one might assume. Simply telling someone "the answer" rarely works. The first reason for this is because you may be trying to explain a principle to someone with which they have no familiarity at all. For example, "Love," is a nice word, but what if the person has never experienced real love in their life? It is hard to have any meaning until there is an experience to go with it.

This means that sometimes you are in a kind of Helen Keller situation. As the pastor, you are helping someone to learn the language of heaven, but you may be teaching that language from nothing, relying solely on what the other person does know. How can you do that? You could talk about the qualities of love, but that is like talking about life in another country. It is very hard to grasp if they have never been there. Fortunately, Jesus had the same problem. He was from heaven and had to communicate heavenly truth to a people who had never experienced it. So you must use the same tools that Jesus did— analogies and stories from this world.

Stories and analogies are helpful tools because people don't always want to hear the truth. Nathan the prophet was confronted with this situation in 2 Samuel 12. David was deep in sin, and God sent Nathan to correct him. Rather than open fire and just tell David that he was in grave sin, God had Nathan use a story—an analogy which would generate the right emotional response for David—which then could be used to open his eyes. God relies on stories throughout the Bible because people are much blinder concerning themselves than they are concerning others. The nature of sin is that we give ourselves a pass and are harsh toward others. Therefore if you tell a story, a person will very often be able to see exactly what is wrong, like David did. It can be a way of helping them see their own behavior more clearly.

This was Jesus' main method of helping people come to the truth. Anyone who has read the New Testament knows that Jesus used a lot of stories and analogies. In fact, He did it so much that the disciples complained He was not being plainspoken enough. Sometimes it seemed that Jesus was being cagey, like some Eastern sage, but there was a method to the madness. It has to do with the fact that we are deaf. Sin causes us to be unable to hear. We can physically hear words of course, but the ability to really understand the realities of God makes no natural sense to us because of the thick sludge of sin.

Stories are therefore a powerful teaching tool in your arsenal—either yours or someone's you know. A person may not be able to see their own flaws, but they can easily spot the same flaw in someone else. It is important that you do not share names or use a story from anyone you are actively working with, but sharing an anonymous story from a past experience can be very powerful, i.e. "There was a guy I knew once who did [X]." This can help someone see in a lot more color what they are doing, especially if the story is dramatic. For example, a friend of mine who married a supermodel ended up divorced partly because he didn't know how to be real with others. He felt he had to keep up appearances. His testimony makes a great story because it teaches the importance of being real. It teaches how you can have everything but still be empty and heading for the rocks.

A second kind of story you can use is a personal confession. Jesus obviously didn't have anything to confess in that sense, but the rest of us do. We all have stories of things we've struggled with and tried to overcome. The way you tell it matters. If you come off as though you've just got a quick answer or solution, or like you are this amazing guy now that you have everything figured out, then your story will backfire. Your story needs to be told with humility, like you're sharing with a friend. Do not share a lot of personal stories with people who will see it as weakness. Only share them with people who can appreciate and resonate with them. Someone who is prideful or immature will just think your story means they are better than you, foolishly failing to realize that this kind of thinking is exactly why they are still at square one.

A third kind of story is an abstract analogy. Using some kind of comparison is very powerful if you can find one that is relevant to that person. Jesus talked to an agrarian society so He used a lot of sheep analogies, and cooking, and grain. He mixed in some banking and war stories for the more political urban types. So I might talk to a construction worker about framing a house, or tell an athlete about moving a ball down the field. I need to speak your language. I may only know a little about framing a house, but when I say it, it conjures up something very rich for the hearer. Jesus may have never herded sheep Himself, but He could see how similar it was to what God wanted for His people. I try all kinds of analogies looking for the ones that stick most or communicate best to that person. Once I have something that really sticks, I use it over and over again until they get the depth of it. It's a tool for helping them learn the language of heaven.

Concepts are made real by examples. And examples are given meaning by the concepts. The two go together. If you just give a speech about what the right thing is, it will be hard for the person to really get it. If you just tell a story they will not understand exactly what it means for their life. The Bible and Jesus Himself move from example to principle, and back, all the time. When you tell a story, especially a real story, it makes things real to someone. When you give the moral of the story with a good example, it becomes something they can take with them everywhere.

GIVING CORRECTION

In the first church I was in, correction was a staple of pastoral care. The stories of senior pastors correcting others in deep sin were astonishing to me. They were gutsy and macho, and it seemed to work. Over time I learned, however, that the church culture I was in was high on correction, and low on love. The pastors would correct you, but you didn't usually feel they had any personal investment or love toward you. This led me to be luke-warm on the whole idea of being corrected or giving correction, even though I got my fair share. A lot of people think this way, I believe. They're burned out on authority.

With enough time in the other chair, however, I've started to really see how important correction is. The question is, how do you know when to correct someone? And how do you do it in love?

Giving correction, especially in our contemporary "live and let live" American culture, may seem extremely difficult — especially if you have the "I really love you" pastor's heart discussed at the beginning of this book. Secular counseling models usually refrain from the idea of giving correction at all. The counselor is sup-posed to ask questions and help you make decisions for yourself according to your own values. There is no absolute morality to ground things.

On the other extreme, the so-called Biblical Counseling movement is entirely centered around giving correction. Rebuking you with a Bible verse and telling you to repent is the fundamental idea. I heard the story of a man who went to get counseling under this model and came back the second week for help. On the second week the pastor simply asked him, "I told you last week it was a sin...Did you repent yet?" I find this completely absurd. If that's what "counseling" and "pastoral care" are, then skip it. Just read Deuteronomy and Jeremiah a few times instead, and that will help you repent. A real pastor is supposed to help you know what to repent of, help you see it and turn away from it, and then help you live it out. If someone is so fundamentally lacking in mercy that they can't see that, they have no business being a pastor.

The very first rule of correction is contained in that oh-so-highly-corrective epistle of James 1:20: "The anger of man does not work the righteousness of God." If you are angry with some-one, or frustrated with them, and then you give them correction, you will get negative results. You cannot produce the fruit of righteousness in them through human anger. I have learned that when am frustrated or angry with someone, they actually go deaf. They simply do not hear anything I say. All they hear is, "Will is angry with me," which normally leads to, "*He* has a problem, not me." As soon as you get angry, you become the problem. Correction therefore, in order to be heard properly, must be given in love. You have to be wanting the best for your person, and wanting them to escape their sin and all of its problems, before your words will be heard.

This means that when you give correction, what you are usually doing is simply truth telling. You're going to say something which might make them very upset, but the anger should come from them, not from you—i.e. I'm not mad at you for your sin, but you may be mad at me for telling you the truth about it. If you become good at this, you can actually say things which would normally be very confrontational yet create no confrontation. I believe this kind of correction reflects the heart of God. He corrects us without anger all the time, just by telling the truth. If He were angry with us every time we sinned, He would be angry all the time. Instead the Bible says that He is "slow to anger and abounding in love" (Psalm 103:8). God always looks for the best and sees the best, and in order to be a good reflection of Him, you have to as well.

The second rule of correction is that some people need more than others. I have four children. One requires a lot of intensity to get through. My younger two will usually adjust their behavior at even the simplest suggestion. God says that a "bruised reed He will not break." (Isa 42:3). In Psalm 18:25-26 we see that God responds to people according to the attitude of their hearts.

To the faithful you show yourself faithful,

To the blameless you show yourself blameless,

To the pure you show yourself pure,

But to the devious you show yourself shrewd.

When someone is in a posture of humility and vulnerability, a forceful word will crush them. But when someone is prideful and deaf, you might have to "shout" for them to hear you at all. To that person, little suggestions are not heard at all. James and John got a mild word suggesting they reconsider what spirit they were of (Luke 9:55). Peter, a bit of a tougher character, got a direct rebuke for harboring Satan (Matthew 16:23). But the Pharisees, the most prideful and hardened of all, got lengthy castigations which probably included Jesus bring quite a bit of emotional force (Matthew 23).

Jesus loved all people but brought more or less force as was most likely to get through to them. Most of us have difficulty using different levels of volume. Either you are naturally a cowboy and do well dealing with Pharisees, or you are a dove and do well with the broken-hearted. A great pastor learns to deal well with both, growing in the area where he is weakest and applying different volume as needed.

Correction should also be more about who you are than what you did. Another way of saying this is, your attitude is more important than your behavior. God wants you to take responsibility for what you do, but the significance of that is really about Him exposing who you are. The fact that you walked out on your wife is bad, but the focus of our discussion should not be to punish you for that, but to help you become the kind of person that would not have walked out on her in the first place. This includes dealing with the past, but the focus is on the present so you can create a better future.

When I give correction, I prefer to rely on what I know a person is already convicted about. Usually they have made statements already about it, and how it is impacting others. Those kinds of statements are the best way to correct someone. Reflect their own words back to them so that they see what they are doing and that they need to stop. Bring clarity about the consequences of what they are doing. It's not about you saying "no." It is about them seeing exactly where their pattern of thinking or behavior is going. By talking about consequences, I am able to maintain the posture of love and friendship while I deliver a hard message.

In only a few cases have I ever had to correct someone because they are completely off the reservation and unaware of what they are doing. If someone persists in serious error after being warned repeatedly in this way, you should discontinue the relationship. This is a form of excommunication. Tell them to call you when they are ready to get serious with God. This is not a step to be taken lightly but it is one that you must sometimes take, otherwise your relationship will simply serve to validate them in their sin.

Finally, is the rule that you should use correction sparingly. When someone actually hears correction, it can be very disorienting and a bit depressing. I know it is for me! Even with a lot of practice, it's hard to receive correction rightly. I have to work it through with God, feel bad about it for awhile, and then regain my balance. Because I take it seriously, I have to let it work its way through my entire personality, changing what God wants me to change. Therefore, if someone receives your correction seriously, you have to then switch postures— you move from the oppositional stance, to coming along side and helping them live out their new life direction. You are helping them overcome their sin, rather than forcing them to see it over and over.

WHAT TO ADDRESS?

Sometimes when a person comes to you it seems they have all kinds of confusing problems wrapped up together. It can be hard to figure out what angle to start with or where to focus. Remember, the foundation of everything you are going to accomplish is based connecting the person with God. That's when the person will get real help. Things you say or do for them may have a temporary effect, but the long term help they need is for you to help them get plugged into the life which flows from Jesus. That is why this is priority one. Once you get through the first wave of whatever they brought to the table, your first ministry goal is to help them connect to the head, which is Christ.

For many people this begins with the simple understanding that God loves them very deeply and wants to help solve their problem. He doesn't cause them. Between popular religious doctrine and the sinfulness of the human heart, it is extremely common for people to blame God rather than take responsibility for their situation. Sometimes correcting this is as simple as you giving them a new perspective, but other times there will more complex reasons why they cannot accept it. Since this is the fundamental basis for all successful counseling, all other issues are secondary until this issue is resolved.

Beyond this, it is important to focus on what the Holy Spirit is dealing with. You are the mouthpiece of the love of God, not quote-a-Scripture. As you look into the person's life, what is the area that most needs changing? What area is God clearly working in already? What are the areas where they are suffering or feeling conviction? Those are the areas you should speak to.

All of us, if Jesus were to show up today and address everything wrong about us would crumble into dust. Focus on the major area where God wants to see a change. If they change that area, all kinds of other little things will resolve themselves, and God may bring up a new area later. If you start correcting every little thing, you will put the person into legalism and end up controlling their lives. Essentially you will take over the role of the Holy Spirit and misrepresent the character and grace of God. What God wants to do in the big areas of their life will get drowned out with your tips on cutting back their donut intake.

In the same respect, less is more when you are talking to the person. When you share things, make it short and then pause to see if they get it. Ask them, "Does that make sense?" or, "Do you see that?" Give them an opportunity to reflect on what you are telling them. Remember, preaching a sermon is not going to change them. They have heard lots of those already. Neither is going off about multiple topics so they lose the first points you told them.

Resist the urge to reshape their entire life as well. When you become hands-on in someone's life, this can all too easily happen. You are not there to tell them whether to fast or not, or what job to take. Your job is to focus on the operating system of their walk with God. Sure, occasionally you can comment if asked, but in general it's a good idea to avoid those areas. This is firstly because it can become controlling quickly. Either the person will like this kind of input and ask for more, or they will not like it, then get offended, and shut the process down. Secondly, then you're on the hook for the results. They should be responsible for their actions and decisions, not you. You're not even there to stop them from doing wrong things. You should warn them if they are going to make a major mistake, but your focus is on the reasons why they are making their decisions. Most people are more attached to the fruit of their problems than the roots anyway. If you can cut the roots, the fruit will simply just die.

Secondly, if you get too deeply into the details you might find yourself shutting down what God wants to do. I might give someone a book to read, but I'm not going to expect them to follow my personalized reading plan for their life. I am very careful not to touch areas where God might be working in their lives. For example, unless someone is clearly fasting because of legalism, I will never question it. If they like to run from conference to conference to encounter God, even if I feel it is unbalanced, I don't touch it. I don't try to bring someone into direct agreement with me theologically either, aside from the points that become relevant and focal during a session such as the love and goodness of God. I try to keep the main thing the main thing.

PRAYER

Other than the ministry of truth, the ministry of prayer is crucial. Prayer is very powerful and very important to a successful counseling session. You should never leave a session without praying. When you feel the Holy Spirit wanting to "cut in" and interrupt what you am doing, stop. Begin to minister instead.

When a person is in a posture of prayer, they enter a state of extreme vulnerability. This is a place where you can partner with God to do real surgery on their identity. Because of this vulnerability, it is important that you never use prayer as a way of praying correction over them. Prayer time is when you can prophetically help them bring things to the surface and encounter God's love. If you get something corrective while in prayer, stop for a minute. Open your eyes, ask questions, or go back to the ministry of truth.

There are several kinds of prayer ministry which can be effective during a session.

Love Breakthrough. The love breakthrough is the most important kind of prayer ministry you will do. You need to help the person connect with God's love for them. First, instruct them in the truth about God's attitude toward them—He's all-loving, all-forgiving, and always ready to help you. Then help them take action on it. The simplest way to do this is to have them put on some worship music and try to imagine if God loved them perfectly. In order to bypass intellectual objections, I tell people to simply pretend it were true that God perfectly loved them all the time. Put on some intimate worship music, step out of the room, and give them a piece of paper. Tell them to imagine God's perfect love coming toward them and to write down any reason why God can't love them. After a few minutes come back and check in. They might need coaching, or you might need to address some things on the paper. If they are having trouble, ask them to imagine any time when they felt close to God, or imagine what perfect love might be like. The point is to help them get an experience with God that you can build on in the future. Usually you can tell when someone finally receives the love breakthrough. It is worth it.

Repentance Prayer. Prayers of repentance are not simply when people say "I repent of [X]." That is an important step, but making the words real involves something happening in the heart. A person has to turn away from sin and toward the love of God, or bring the sin and pain into the presence of God so that He can heal it. Whenever something painful comes up in a counseling session, there may be an opportunity for a prayer of repentance. You might combine this with some ministry of truth to help them turn away from sin and toward God. The key thing, however, is that this remains an experience. As they bring their sin to God, they should experience an exchange. A part of them that was dark can be filled with God's light. I like to thank God that the person is severed from their sin once they have confessed and repented— that the sin is over, it's done, it's separated from them. Pray with them to help them achieve the exchange.

Thread Ministry. This is a special kind of repentance and healing that goes deeper. For difficult and intractable areas, it may be a good idea to work with the person to bring forward formative memories which helped shape their perspective on a given issue. Do they have deep wounds or moments when they hardened their heart toward God or others? Ask God to bring forth moments from their past (or present) and minister to those areas. Once these broken memories come forward, the way to address them is to "repair" them. For example, if they feel like their mother wasn't there for them, have them forgive their mother and imagine God's perfect love and care are coming in at that point in their life. Let it sink in deep and move to the next experience. This kind of prayer will help them rewire their inner emotional DNA and see their life differently.

Deliverance Prayer. Deliverance prayer is when you become aggressive toward the devil to tell him to leave. Deliverance is not a focus of my ministry, but it is still an important component. If you start to tap into certain roots, a demon may manifest. If he does, you should cast him out. Someone who is coming for counseling and has this problem usually needs to repent of various things in order to remove the devil, however. It is different than a person who has no control over their faculties. The demon is usually there due to being welcomed in some way. This means you may need to lead the person in a process of repentance of sin which is associated with that demon. If the devil does not go the first time you pray, do not be discouraged. As you continue to minister to the issues of a person's heart, you will weaken its hold and it will have to go.

Prophetic Prayer. A good counselor should be practiced in the prophetic. This does not mean that you have to be getting names and phone numbers out of the glory cloud. It means you need to be able to tap in to what God is saying about the person's situation as you pray. Often when I begin to pray for someone, a new line of idea or counsel will come to me. Sometimes I get an insightful analogy I would have never thought of ordinarily. This can release a fresh perspective from which you can apply the other techniques. For example, you may discover that a person is harboring anger towards someone, and then you can go back and address that.

Prophetic prayer can be aggressive. It's not always just warm fuzzy information. When someone is feeling deeply oppressed, or cannot pray for themselves, I may rise up and speak the truth forcefully over them. This is designed to help them break the emotional weight which is holding them back, and push away any demonic oppression which might also be involved.

Activation Prayer. An activation prayer is where you help the person break a box. They may feel hemmed in, timid, or simply need a little push to take control of their life. Instead of just praying "over" the person, as is very common in church circles, you give them the reigns of the prayer and coach them from the sidelines. You try to get them to get aggressive about the truth, against the devil, or more generally declaring God's will over their lives. You may need to guide them in what to say, how to say it, or have them repeat it until they can say it with conviction. This is especially necessary for more reserved personality types, but be careful that you do not push someone too far at once.

This summarizes just a few of the primary ways that prayer is integral to the counseling process. Of course, more fundamentally, during the entire session you need to be in communion with God to see where it is going. What does He want to highlight or focus on? The entire process is like getting someone out of a maze. It is like they are trapped in a certain part of a maze with lots of dead ends and will bounce out of one dead end and into another. You are helping them find the true way out, and that requires God.

Reflection Questions

1. Do you already use stories in your counseling, or do you think that they need to remain private for some reason? What about analogies? Try to use one in a conversation with a friend or family member and see if it helps them.

2. What is your experience with correction? How do you employ it in your own home? Do you have a bitter taste in your mouth about it from your past or from church experience? Can you see it in a redemptive way?

3. What is your track record on reshaping others' lives? Do you tend to give too much input and advice? Do you like to give people game-plans to get their lives right? Why doesn't this work out?

4. If you are not familiar with the types of prayer ministry listed, get more information or have someone mature actually pray for you in these different ways so you can learn it.

Action

Your ministry time with someone may be dramatic and miraculous, or it may be just some basic conversation. Either way, you need to remember that pastoral care is a long term process, and that process is in the hands of the person, not you. A major issue may take a few months for a motivated person to work through, and someone's entire life takes years to overhaul. Sometimes people come to you for help believing that talking is enough, but what really matters is that their lifestyle changes and they do things to activate the truth.

This is where the action plan comes in. Just like you never leave a session without prayer, never leave a session without homework. What is the logical way to build on the fresh perspective or breakthrough they got that week? They don't need a long list of do's and don'ts. Just look for one item you can give them to take action on before you meet the next time.

- This may be a resource for them to review such as a book, youtube clip, or DVD.

- It may be a lifestyle change, such as spending 15 minutes a day receiving God's love.

- It may be taking steps to redefine a relationship, such as calling home to have a heart to heart, or getting honest with a spouse.

- It may be an activity, such as exploring wounded areas in prayer with God.

- If it is a pattern of sin, it may be joining a group or introducing them to some other kind of mentor relationship.

Whatever the action is, it should be logical and achievable. You are not trying to build Rome in a day, you are just trying to activate the ministry steps you took. As you take single steps in the right direction, this will have impacts on all kinds of other areas of their life.

You may have noticed what is not on the list. I do not generally give Bible studies or other rote activities as homework. As a pastor, your job is to help make the Bible real. If they were able to make Scriptures work on their own, they wouldn't be coming to you. You are helping them develop a living relationship with God and so the homework needs to reflect the real, living dimension of His Spirit inside them.

Another reason why homework is important is because it determines if they are really going to work for their freedom or not. In general, I do not meet with someone a second time until they have taken the action we discussed the first time. If they don't make any effort, then meeting together is a waste of time. You will just end up repeating the first session's lessons and feeling like you need to do more to make something happen. Christians often come expecting a ministry session to be magic. In reality, the ministry session is like a rudder, designed to help change the course of the ship. It is only in the process of sailing the ship, however, that things really change.

There is action on your part as well. When God gives someone into your care as pastor, it is your responsibility to follow up. You need to check in on the person every once in a while. This is an art. If you follow up too much then you are taking the initiative of the relationship and trying to make them grow. If you do not do it at all, they may be too easily distracted and drawn away. I think of the outreach like a "ping." I call or text or reach out and see how much receptivity there is to continuing the growth process together. Sometimes people flake out, but sometimes they simply max out on what they can benefit from for a while. In those cases, I let the relationship go onto the back burner until God brings it back to life again. Perhaps they have made a choice to fundamentally reject sound counsel and it is time to let them walk out that decision. If they were being driven to it by their idol, then they will usually be back.

The point is that I will "ping" to give the person an easy opportunity to receive more ministry and reset the level of investment and relationship. If someone is in crisis, I want them to feel like I am there "on call" to help them. Sometimes my action will be to invade their life to help break them out of a pit, but I do not make this the norm. It is important that my level of energy and effort match what they are ready to put in and receive.

There is a positive aspect to the pastoral counseling relationship that shouldn't be neglected either. Because the process of getting closer to God involves dealing with sin, bondage, and lifetraps, it's easy for that to become the focus. But pastoral care is not just about dealing with sin and bondage all of the time. It's about helping people avoid pitfalls which the devil has set to arrest their development, so they can grow and reach their potential. Once the person moves past crisis mode, if your relationship is good, they will continue to seek you for other things. In this phase, your relationship changes and become more rewarding. Instead of being Pastor 911, you become a ministry coach. Instead of talking about the bad, you start to help them with the good. And eventually, if you did a really good job, the person you were pastoring may surpass you or become a ministry peer. This is the sign of true success, a rare reward for the difficult and sometimes thankless job of showing love through pastoral care.

RESOURCES

Your resource library is an important part of your arsenal as pastor. What resources do you have which you can recommend which will help the person attack various problems? Start by thinking about each of the books, sermons or movies which helped you take major steps in your walk and what role they played. In other words, don't think about what is hip at the moment, think about it from a specifically pastoral angle – which resources helped you grow and why? This set of resources is the foundation of your pastoral tool belt. Then branch out. Talk to those you trust as mature Christians and ask them which resources helped them grow, to get more ideas. Working as part of a pastoral team helps in grown this list. Each part of the pastoral team will know and have benefitted from different resources and you will be able to bounce ideas off one another.

When you recommend a resource, you have to be sensitive to what will lead that person off track. I do not mean that the resource is perfect or that you agree with every last word in the book. What I mean is something more specific – when you give someone a resource, you are doing so to help them grow, to break a box they have. The nature of the human heart is to latch onto those things which reinforce the box we are already in. So if you give someone a book that is 90% truth, and 10% error to someone who is trying to get free from error, you will find that they often latch onto the 10% which reinforces their particular issue. I have found that some books which helped me personally are counter productive for people I am pastoring because they get hung up on some confusing aspect, which for me personally was not an issue.

For example if I were to read a book on the seed principle of faith, I might filter out aspects which teach you to love and crave money, but someone else may interpret the book as being entirely about getting rich. That means in a pastoral role, I pay close attention to how effective resources are at helping someone grow and whether or not the person is likely to "choke on the bones" or not. Some of our favorites for personal growth include:

- Most of the books and sermons of Dr. Jim Richards of Impact ministries. Almost no one is better at helping someone really get honest, break religion, and deal with the issues of the heart.

- Although I don't use them myself I have observed good pastoral fruit from those who listen to Dan Mohler sermons.

- Of course, I give my own book, *Free at Last* out quite frequently, not because I am self-promoting, but because it is specifically designed to help a person confront the main issues holding them back in God.

- R.T. Kendall has a great book on *Total Forgiveness.*

- Andrew Murray's books on *Total Surrender* and *Humility*

- *Holiness, Truth and the Presence of God* by Frangipane

- Books by Cloud and Townsend, especially *Boundaries*

- Books by Gary Chapman, especially for marriage *The Five Love languages*

- Roberts Liardon sermons or books. They are very practical and straightforward

- For issues related to healing, Curry Blake's Divine Healing Technician series

- Michael Brown books.

There are two tendencies popular in most mainstream resources which I consider to be counter productive, and that is why I am always on the lookout for good ones: The first is an overemphasis on identity or confession to the point where sin is never dealt with. This leads people to ignore heart issues and think they are much more mature than they really are. The second is the tendency to emphasize the sovereignty of God. This leads people to be passive, blame God, or wait for Him to do things.

There is a difference between what is exciting and what makes you grow. As a pastor, what you are looking for are things that will help a person grow. At the same time, they have to actually resonate with the kind of person you are pastoring. I don't give people resources because they are "deep" but because they work. If someone comes back confused, it drops off the list. If you have books or resources that you find helpful from a pastoral perspective, please contact me because I want to hear from you

Reflection Questions

1. Consider the resources—books, audios, videos—you have in your possession, what issues they are good for, and if you need to purchase some additional items to hand out to those you minister.

Part III – Perspectives You Need

Shaped by Your Family

In this section, I am going to deal with several very common issues which arise again and again in contemporary culture. By understanding how these issues shape the person you are dealing with, you will have the proper framework from which to counsel. The first and most fundamental is the family.

Family is the context in which every person comes to understand human relationships and, by extension, human identity. If something is wrong in your family, something is wrong in you. And vice versa — if something is wrong in you, almost certainly, you can find its roots in your family experience.

Before I launch too deeply into this topic, I want to make clear that what I believe is distinct from Freudian psychology which finds all pathologies in childhood. It's also distinct from popular Charismatic psychology, which building off of Freud, looks to your parents and family to blame them for your shortcomings. Let's be clear: sin is the ultimate root of all your shortcomings. If you could have a perfect family who never did anything wrong, you would still struggle with sin. I will even take it one step further: the people who blame their parents the most are usually the ones whose parents did the most to bend over backwards for them.

Therefore, what we're talking about here is not about how mom and dad caused all your problems — sin is the root of your problems. What we're really talking about here is how the specific patterns of relationship, and also patterns of sin, took root in your upbringing. While there are a myriad of ways issues can be formed through your upbringing, I want to focus on those rooted in the structure of the family itself. Since we live in an era of the disintegration of the Biblical family, you will encounter these patterns over and over again.

The first and foremost thing to observe about family is that when God created the world, He made a man and a woman. He drew the woman from out of the man's flesh and set them together in the garden as a couple perpetually. From the union of this couple came children. These children inherited their identity from their parents. In other words, God made the stable, two-biological parent family where the parents love each other, and the man is the head, is the normal, healthy way to grow up. This used to be the norm in our culture, and in most of Western culture for more than 1000 years. But now that is coming to an end, and all around you will find unending alternative arrangements. While those in these situations do the best they can, it should be recognized that anything less than God's original pattern leaves a child with gaps—some of them severe.

When you are pastoring someone, you need to be aware of this. In order for someone to have a different future, deep things about their identity which began in childhood have to be rewritten. If you've never known love, or you were abandoned, or you never had a father figure, these things have a profound impact on your view of yourself and of the world. The very definition of love, the filters through which you experience every interaction, are significantly altered. Let's review some of these alternative situations and how they impact the person that is formed.

The upside-down family. Due to feminism, this is an extremely common family type. The woman is in some way the head of the family. The man is more passive, or feels like he always has to negotiate with the mother. The woman is tough and shows less emotion, the man is soft and more emotional. This family is upside-down. God created woman to be softer and dependent on the man, not vice versa. Furthermore, God made the woman from the man. He was first, and she was created as a companion. I will explore this more in a separate section on gender identity and formation, but the point here is that when a family is upside-down, the person formed from that family is also upside down. Daughters become tough and dominant, and sons become soft and dependent. These positions are unnatural to the way God made us, and therefore cause collateral problems. Men from this situation will need to learn to be tough and brave, and women will need to learn to be submissive and vulnerable.

Single-parent family. A single parent can provide many things for a child, but can really only manifest one aspect of God's identity. It's hard for mom to be dad too, or dad to be mom too. More importantly, the child cannot see love that flows back and forth modeled for them. They often feel like the center of the single parent's world, instead of part of a bigger world. I think of how my little girl instinctively always comes to get in the middle of the hug when mommy and daddy are together. She knows she is a part of something. She gets certain things from her mom and certain complementary things from her dad, and she gets a sense of warmth and safety growing up in the middle of the two. Not having this creates gaps. But a good single parent home is actually overall not as deficient as some other situations, especially when it is supplemented by grandparents or extended family to help fill the missing gaps.

The divorced (and usually remarried) family. Divorce, as everyone knows, is like splitting a child in two. It is literally impossible for a divorce not to fundamentally damage a child. You feel safe and secure knowing you have a mom and a dad and they love each other, and then suddenly one of them is gone and they don't love each other. It leaves a void in your soul. Then one or more of the parents gets remarried and you're part of what is now called a "blended" family. You are living with someone who is not your mom or not your dad, but is playing that kind of role. You might reject their authority in your life, and they might in turn treat you like a "stepchild" — not quite as loved and as good as their own children. Sometimes it's malicious, but usually it's really just the natural way things work. It's hard to be the mom or dad of kids that aren't your own and aren't bonded to you in that from-birth kind of way.

Furthermore, the step-parent always feels secondary to the biological parent, whose love the child naturally craves even if the biological parent was a wastrel. Some families are able to make this work better than others or form two relatively healthy families for the child to go between. Usually, however, it's not really that great of a situation. Isolation, brokenness, and emotional shutdown are all fruits of these situations. Sometimes suspicion of the opposite gender, or marriage, occurs. Blended families can compensate for divorce reasonably well, but usually it leaves a significant scar.

Serial partners. If someone divorces and remarries once, that's one thing, but if they go through a series of partners, that leads to a much more damaging situation. Short-term partners are even less committed and caring that the step-parent. They might even abuse the child or the parent. The biological parent might neglect the child for the attention of boyfriends or girlfriends. It's an overall very neglected way to grow up and leads people to think they are worthless or in the way. A person from this situation usually has an array of traumas and emotional blockages to unwind.

Abandonment or double-rejection. All of the above alternative families, however, are fortunate compared to the child who is actually abandoned by one or both of their parents. When a child is abandoned, or rejected to the point that they might as well be abandoned, it leaves deep scars. The sense of worthlessness, anger, of being unlovable, pervades their identity. This person experiences the world very differently than everyone else — almost like being on the outside looking in. Everyone else seems to be "normal" while this person craves what everyone else is taking for granted — people that love them unconditionally and won't throw them in the garbage. Even when you give this person love, they can't really receive it because they believe deep inside that they are worthless.

Permissive Parents. A generation ago, everyone talked about parents as being too strict, but now the pendulum has swung the other way. It is extremely rare to encounter anyone under 50 years old from a two-parent home whose parents were overly strict. And while abusive families today get a lot of press, the most common family in America right now has parents who are too permissive. This leads to the self-centered or ungrateful child with little to no conscience. They are always the victim.

Making it worse, in such homes parents may allow rivalries and feuds between children that can lead to a variety of imbalances. They either become an overachiever who thinks too highly of themselves and steals the spotlight, or they become an underachiever who feels like they can never live up to the spotlight of their sibling. The overachiever will be prideful about their amazing gifts, because no one ever put them in their place, and the underachiever will be selfish because no one ever confronted them and made them aware of how their behavior affects others.

Disconnected Parents. Another major kind of problem you will encounter from two-parent homes is when the relationship between the two parents is fundamentally unhealthy or unloving. They are both there, but instead of working together as a team, or at least presenting it that way to the children, they play the children off of one another, use mockery as a form of correction, or just do not model love to the children. Sometimes these parents are just staying together "for the children." But you can feel the emotion divorce. Other times one parent is a Christian and the other is not—they just "live and let live."

The way the mother-father relationship is modeled will dictate a lot to the child about what it means to be in a relationship. If parents don't trust one another, the grown up child may not trust. If their parents are not vulnerable or do not communicate, the child may not learn to either. One of the most unhealthy characteristics picked up from the unloving family is that it's bad to be emotionally vulnerable. They don't experience a flow of love between their parents that they can be a part of, and often they might be in the middle of a power play between the two parents. A two-parent family that is broken to the extent that the couple is together in name only, can be just as damaging as a broken family.

These are just a few patterns under which a seemingly infinite number of situations can arise. The point of highlighting them is to help you understand that when you minister to someone, you are ministering to their family life. Exploring the dynamics which caused them to think and relate the way that they do is a very important part of walking to freedom. The situations lurking in their past are also often sources of present pain. This is why one of the first items for conversation with someone, once you move beyond the initial issues, should be about their family experience. You want to understand what models of love (or gap of love) they experienced. The greater the gaps, the more significant the work required to help them live a new kind of life.

In my experience, it takes many years of hard work on the part of the person as well as the counselor to really rewrite the impact of a bad upbringing. Parenting sunk in for about twenty years, and so changing this programming does not happen overnight. The good news is that God can use you while you are on the journey. In fact, He loves to show Himself through those were orphaned or rejected in childhood. He is the perfect parent, the universal adopter. And He can use damaged people for His glory while they press through. God's dictate isn't "Become perfect and then serve the Lord." It is "Walk with me as I heal you."

Reflection Questions

1. Do you subscribe to the "generational curse" theology or any other theology which blames parents for the sins of the children? How is this different from the idea that your relationship patterns are learned in childhood?

2. Did you come from any of these alternative family situations? Have you gotten healing from any wounds related to that?

The Gender Lie

One of the most potent lies in America today is that men and women are the same. I don't mean equal, I mean *the same*. Feminism is based on the idea that gender is socially constructed — you act female just because you were raised to; you were brought up to be weak in an oppressive male-dominated environment. Feminism teaches that if we can overthrow this, all of the world's problems including violence and war will be solved. This was widely believed in our culture for nearly 40 years, and is only recently starting to be seen as the falsehood it is. No culture at any time in history has believed men and women are the same because it's manifestly not true.

Men and women act differently because of reasons that are biological not just socially constructed. Nevermind the fact that God actually created man and woman from different materials, just take a look at biology. Consider testosterone. Men are born with a lot of it, and it does all kinds of things to your development. It makes you assertive, focused, and driven. It gives men muscles and a higher sex drive. Then there's the brain. Women have a wider corpus collosum, which allows the two halves of their brain to work together better than a man's more linear mind. They also bear children, obviously, and have a different physiology to accommodate what pertains to that. Although many people even in the secular world are beginning to realize the folly of androgyny, you may have been brought up under this false and damaging belief that men and women are created the same. And you will definitely encounter those who have been negatively affected by it. Part of what you are doing when you are counseling is helping to restore people to their God-given gender identity and to embrace it.

The idea that men and women are naturally different dovetails with the idea that God created us to be complementary. The second principle of feminism was that men and women are the same, but women are superior. Although this is a logical contradiction, it's what is believed and taught through media and education. I remember in first grade having a conversation with a girl in my class that went something like this:

Her: (mockingly) "Anything a man can do, women can do better."

Me: (stunned) "Well you can't have babies without boys."

Her: (snidely) "We're working on it."

As this exchange illustrates, erasing the God-given need for a man is the heart of feminism. The truth is that men and women are different, and God created us to play complementary roles. Neither one is superior, but both are necessary. In some areas men have strengths, and in some areas women have strengths. When put together, the two complement one another and fulfill God's purposes.

The fallout from feminism is suffocated men and stressed out women. Since it's not culturally acceptable to praise masculinity, that means a whole generation of men has grown up starved for affirmation. To suggest that women are better than men is completely acceptable in our culture, but to suggest that men might be "better" than women in some way is like swearing. So our men have stopped believing in manhood, and they've stopped acting like men. At the same time, feminism has wounded women by telling them that since they are better than men, and gender is a socially constructed prison cell, they have to be and do everything to prove it. A whole generation of girls has grown up under the pressure to have an awesome career, stay absolutely gorgeous, and be the amazing, nurturing mom of two kids while fixing the kitchen sink. Not just *can* you do it all, you *should* do it all.

The net effect of these pressures is predictable. Men were told they are good for nothing, so they act like it. Women were told they have to be everything, so they act like it. In addition, men were told they need to be more in touch with their emotions since masculinity is the cause of all problems. Women were told they need to toughen up to win in the hard-edged man's world. So now we have a generation of women who can't cry and men who won't stop. Women are feeling overwhelmed and craving strong men all the more, now that none are to be found. Men are baffled as to why being sweet and sensitive hasn't made them an attractive mate. Bad boys get the girls because at least they act like men!

If you look carefully, what you'll see is that feminism leads to a complete inversion of God's design. God created the woman from the man. He made the man stronger and more driven naturally. He made the man to be the leader and the woman to be the supporter. He made the man edgy and less sensitive to criticism, and he made the woman more aware of others and wanting to please them. He is resolute, she is more pliable.

Is this hard for you to read? It's only because we live in post-feminist America where we believe in myths. Many men will respond by saying, "Well, I'm a man but I'm sensitive and in touch with my emotions." And women will protest that their sons were born sensitive and their daughters tough. This becomes the evidence that the created order is false — that gender behaviors are just stereotypes. In reality these kinds of statements are evidence of how far our culture has drifted from the created order. It's not about personality—it's about roles God created to prosper His family.

To really fulfill God's model, our men need to learn to become strong again, and our women need to learn to become soft again. Men need to learn to control their emotions, and women need to learn to express theirs. Women need to learn to submit to leadership, and men need to learn to act like leaders. This is just not because the Bible gives this model. Even if I were secular, I would say this. The inversion of gender roles is damaging to all parties. We're stuck doing what we're worst at and feeling bad about it instead of doing what we're best at and appreciating what the other person can do.

What does this have to do with pastoral counseling? Well, everyone is dealing with the pressures listed above in some kind of way. It comes up most often in marriage counseling. Not all, but almost all of the marriages I've been involved in fit this upside-down pattern. The man is emotional and the woman is not. Sometimes the woman is driven and the man is not. The woman is the louder, more passionate one in ministry, and the man is not. Women are keyed up and men are checked out. Many times the foundations for these reversed roles were present prior to the marriage but were ignored or affirmed as progressive. Now that the marriage is going on, there are problems. The husband and wife are polarizing one another and neither knows what to do.

To be honest, the church often makes this issue worse rather than better. I think of one man, Dan, who was perfectly masculine until he got saved, and then managed to marry a domineering woman who ended up wanting to kill him. He was then told by his pastors that he was causing the problem by not loving her enough. This bizarre counsel is repeated over and over again by pastors and counselors who are counseling a chauvinistic world that no longer exists. We think it is normal to crack jokes from the pulpit about "checking with the boss" and sermonize our men on how they have to submit to their wives and be more loving. But the contextual message is all wrong. We need to be helping Christian men overcome the lies of feminism that have stolen their masculinity: You are a leader. God made you to protect the woman. She is weaker in important ways that you are strong in. She needs you. You need God's approval, not a woman's approval. God didn't make you to be sensitive, he made you to be strong. He made you for war and that's good.

Not only that, as a side effect, women like a man who has confidence inside himself, instead of one who craves her affirmation. Even women who like to lead or minister want a strong man as a guide. Your role as a counselor is to help men recover or shore up their masculine identity, and that may involve freeing him from messages he is receiving from elsewhere, even the pulpit.

For women, it's a bit different. Only a few women in the church today actually believe the contemporary lie that men are pigs. Those that do have usually been shut down in highly male-dominated environments and have run to feminism as an escape. The average churchgoing woman simply can't figure out why the men are all absent. Most have just taken on all the roles they have been told to, and need help giving some of those back to the men in their lives. They have been told to play the woman and the man, instead of to play the woman and look for a man and help support him in being that. They often find it a relief when you tell them, no, you don't have to be everything. Usually that exposes the underlying trust issues. She takes on all these roles because she has been hurt, or her mother was, and was told not to trust a man and to be tough and steely. The journey for her is to release her from these extra burdens, and help her to trust again, and to realize that it is actually good for her to cry, to be vulnerable and to depend on a man. Many times this is enough to release her from depression, anxiety, anger, control, or any other stress-related problems she's having.

Lastly, it's important to note that partners in marriage usually complement each other. A submissive person will usually marry a dominant, so if the man is passive, he will tend to marry a dominant woman, creating the "upside down" marriage. This can lead to the upside down family because reversed gender identities may pass onto the children. Both parties need to work actively to get their God-given roles back. It takes time and may not be completely achieved, but it a very important part of personal wholeness for everyone.

Reflection Questions

1. What kind of gender roles were embraced in the home you grew up in? Were reverse gender roles supported? Traditional ones complained about?

2. Where do you get your gender identity beliefs today? Do they come from culture, popular science, or Christian books? Do you feel solidified on what the Bible says about the subject?

3. How do "complementary" roles differ from gender "equality?"

Enablement and Boundaries

One of the most common issues that you will encounter in Christian counseling is people that have boundary issues — as in letting themselves get walked on. This is because in Christianity, it's easy to believe Jesus is asking you to be a doormat: turn the other cheek if someone strikes you, give him your shirt if he asks for your coat, love your enemies and pray for those who persecute you. Secular people do not face boundary problems as often because the world's ethic is selfish: how do I meet *my* needs? But in Christianity it is seen as selfish to acknowledge your own needs. You are supposed to be selfless and oriented towards loving others at all times.

This causes enablement problems, or what Christian psychologists Cloud and Townsend have called problems with "boundaries." The basic anatomy of the problem is that a Christian feels that he or she must keep helping or being in relationship with someone who is hurting them. They feel that they do not have the right to say no or defend themselves. What I like to point out to people of this mentality is that submitting to someone who is in sin, is participating in their sin. Do you let someone rape you just because they want to? No, you defend yourself. The first step of getting someone free from enablement is to help them see this basic principle.

Jesus certainly was not teaching that you allow yourself or others to be violated over the long term. He was teaching that we should love in response to evil. I can love and forgive you and yet still believe you should go to prison for your crimes. I can love and forgive you and yet still not allow you back into my life where it hurts. It's not good for me and it's not good for you because *letting you use me only teaches you to sin.* Me loving you requires I let you experience the consequences of your sin instead of me experiencing them. This is because the consequences or the fruit that you sow from your sin are what lead you to repentance. I'm not going to be mean to you or punish you, but I'm also not going to let you put it on me so you can keep sinning.

What enablement does is prevent this cycle of reaping and sowing. Everyone else experiences pain while the sinner enjoys their sinful lifestyle on your expense. It's like you sleeping in the basement while your lazy uncle sleeps in the presidential suite on your dime. You are only helping him perpetuate a fantasy about his life which is not true — that there are no consequences for his selfishness. It's much better that he find it out in this life than in the life to come, when punishment is eternal.

Common patterns in counseling are wives who enable their husbands, parents who enable their children, and moms who overrun boundaries with their kids. Women are natural enablers because they feel bad when they make other people feel bad. That means they want to make other people happy all the time. They will make you happy even if it is making them miserable. They are very prone, therefore, to enabling people in their greed or selfishness.

Husbands, boyfriends, and children are the most likely candidates for this kind of people-pleasing. In the case of a boyfriend, it is the typical abusive pattern where he takes and takes and never gives, and makes her feel bad for not giving more. In the case of a mother, it's usually her putting all her emotional burdens on the daughter and sucking her dry emotionally. In the case of all the children, it is them always demanding and mom never feeling the strength to say 'no.' The solution to this last syndrome is more involvement from a male figure who doesn't mind telling the children no, and will pry the mother away so she can get her own sanity time. Unraveling a woman's enmeshment with her own mother or spouse is significantly more complex. The average wife will want to defend her husband's behavior publicly even when it is killing her on the inside. And the typical daughter is bonded to her mom in a way that is borderline freaky, as if they live in each other's heads! This can be a source of comfort, guidance, and strength when it's healthy, but it can be a really negative thing if it's not.

A tricky thing about conquering enablement with abusive spouses is working with the Christian conscience that you are not supposed to leave a marriage. The abused spouse is in a relationship with someone who is clearly taking advantage of them in serious ways, but they keep going with it because God hates divorce. It gets deeper and deeper until the point where you fear for your life, or you are far away from God or deeply compromised because of your spouse. The fact is that God does not want you in that situation. Your first allegiance is to God, even over your spouse.

I'm not saying to divorce automatically. Many people think divorce is the only option in the case of spousal abuse, but except in the case of physical violence, I actually believe the most Biblical option is separation. It's the classic, "I'm taking the kids to stay with my parents until you work this out." It's that step which lets the other person know that their actions are serious and they are seriously hurting you, but that you are committed to them, that you love them, and that you are not throwing them in the garbage because they failed.

In all but the most severe situations this is a very good option. Sometimes even a weekend alone is enough to bring the spouse back to their senses. And I don't mean that it's a light option. I mean that if your relationship is structurally unhealthy, or there are addiction issues, you should use separation as a way to help rebalance it and assert that you are also an actor in the relationship. They cannot simply put all of the weight on you and take advantage of you. You see? You are giving them a choice from a posture of love. In a truly severe situation of physical abuse, you should get out fast, file divorce and don't look back. This person isn't married to you, they are married to the devil. But in less extreme cases where enablement has caused sin and the doormat situation, separation is a great option.

Enablement not only destroys marriages, it destroys children. Today's culture has most American parents grossly enabling their children in ways that would have shocked our grandparents. We can't tell our kids no for any reason or make them feel bad about anything. This symptom grows and grows until the child has wrecked their life on drugs, is living in your house doing nothing but playing video games, or is in jail, or dead. Parents have to see that their role is to shape the behavior of their children. While kids are little, it is easier. Once the child is older, a shift like that is going to be radical and difficult. An older child who is running the show with their sin might require separation, just like the marriage. From a posture of love you have to let the child know that you will not be doing all of these things to help them sin and bail them out when they do. It's hard because they lash out at you, but it's better for their soul. You do it in love with an open hand, hoping they will learn and come to sanity. Some do, some don't. This kind of separation—financial, emotional, even physical—can be hard for both mothers and fathers. Just remember that unconditional love doesn't mean unconditional support.

Some people simply live their whole lives as enablers and pleasers in all relationships. The problem with this is that when you let everyone have their way, the devil has his way too. When you submit to everyone, you submit to the devil in people. You simply can't make everyone happy. Part of being a Christian actually involves making some people mad. Not because you want to, but because some people always hate the truth. That means you can't be a people pleaser. You have to step away from the demands and expectations of others and stand for the truth, letting their emotions fall where they may. This is putting up a boundary between where they end and you begin.

A boundary is a limit with a choice attached. It says: if you want to be in relationship with me, you can't violate me in this way. You have to be responsible for yourself, and I will be responsible for myself. I'm not going to allow you to take over my emotions and soul. If you do, I will take actions to separate from you. I exercise my free will to move closer to you or farther away as I deem appropriate. Good behavior will be rewarded by closeness and bad behavior will not.

A boundary is a positive thing like the old expression, "Good fences make good neighbors." It doesn't mean we live in isolated bubbles of separation, it just means that when someone overruns your fences all the time, it's time to remind them that it's your property. The neighbors you love can always come through the gate and be welcomed inside. The ones who need boundaries are the ones who jump fences. These are the kind of people who put demands on you and make you feel bad for not meeting them. This might be emotional or it might be financial or otherwise. You can love them but still insist they keep on their side of the fence.

Some people will learn from this, others will simply leave you alone and find someone else to take advantage of.

The bottom line with counseling these kinds of relationships is understanding the basic principle of individual responsibility. People need to assert themselves and separate from those who are sources of unhealthiness in their lives. You will need to take apart people's religious reasons for enabling and show them that in some cases real love means separation or consequences.

Note, you cannot do it for them. It is a foolish mistake to try to make a choice for someone else like telling a wife to separate from her husband or cut off her children. This is why the police do not get involved in domestic violence disputes. You should not either, no matter how much it stirs your conscience. The woman (or man) is feeling bad and so she calls for help so someone else will get this man out of her life. But the fact is that only she can do this. If you get involved, you find that the next day the couple has made up and you are the enemy. Someone who stays in this situation is actually a participant in the sin. The correct thing to do is to coach the person to make their own choice to come out of the sinful relationship. Until they make that choice, there is nothing you can do for them except show them how not making the choice is continuing to hurt everyone including the person they supposedly love. Your role is to show them consequences and give them permission to stop the cycle of pain that being someone else's punching bag causes.

Reflection Questions

1. Have you ever been an enabler in someone else's life, or been a doormat when you should have stood up for yourself? How did it feel? What did you wish?

2. Have you ever been enabled in your own sin by someone who failed to confront you? How did it feel? What did you wish?

3. Think of someone you know for whom some "tough love" would help. Why has no one done it yet? What holds them back?

4. Prepare your heart to answer why "turning the other cheek" does not mean enabling someone to sin.

Conclusion

Pastoral care is an art, and a difficult one. Some nights you will be high because someone got a breakthrough, and other nights you will feel like quitting altogether because someone turned back and fell. After many years of this cycle, I am coming to believe that the only way to avoid it is to fix your eyes upon Jesus. When you love people, you are serving Him. When you reach out to save them, you are extending His hands.

You will see more success as you go, but there will still be many disappointments along the way. This is because often times by the time someone is ready to sit down and get help, they are already in a very bad state. If you derive your self-worth by how well your people do, you will inevitably be depressed. Learn from each experience and each person, but fix your eyes on Jesus. He is the one you are serving and He will reward you for every hand of love you extend, even if it got cut off when you extended it. After all, no one knows better than Jesus what it is like to give love only to have it rejected over and over again. Even to have it fail. When you give love as a pastor, you enter into a kind of fellowship with Jesus that is much deeper than simply receiving. You enter into the fellowship of "God so loved the world."

Although a good pastor puts his or her whole heart into it, you should also recognize that you cannot make decisions another person. You cannot make them repent or connect with God. You can only show them the path.

This booklet was just an introduction into a seemingly endless array of things you will encounter. As I hear from the experiences of others who read it, I want to incorporate your experiences and insights, and I want to hear from you. Please feel free to contact me at will@thegonetwork.net

Made in the USA
Charleston, SC
14 February 2014